Success

It Can Be Yours!

Cathy

I hope you enjoy my story! Be the GURU you are Born to Be;

love
Jerri

Success
It Can Be Yours!

How to be a Millionaire by Using Your Determination

Terri L. Bowersock

TERRI'S
PUBLISHING
& SPEAKING

Published by

Terri's Publishing & Speaking
1826 W. Broadway #4
Mesa, Arizona 85202
(877) 393-5656

Library of Congress Catalog Card Number: 99-97050

ISBN: 0-9676174-0-5

Printed in the United States of America

To people like myself
who have learning disabilities.

Acknowledgments

An extra special thanks to you, Mom, for your love and support. You not only guided me as a child, but went above and beyond when you stuck with me as an adult and helped me find a way to support myself.

To the rest of my parents: Dave and Nancy, and Taw for your love and guidance.

Thanks to my employees, franchisees, and the thousands of customers for your support in building all of my businesses. With a special thanks to my executive team Kevin Crippa, Shelley Santucci, and Marcus Curtis. You are the backbone of the corporation and truly my best friends.

And last, I am grateful to all of those who have helped me, in some way, produce this book. To Reed Rahn for the front cover photo, R&R Studios, Vickie Champion, Kara Rosseaux, Kelly Loeffler, Tamara Coffman, Sue Newberg, Jo-ann Holstein, Lori Schmidt, and my mother, Loretta Bowersock.

contents

My life has been about taking on challenges and setting examples. I did not have a formal education in business, but I have something more important, wisdom and knowledge about it.

I have always enjoyed motivating people to believe in and act on their dreams, spending many hours giving out ideas and encouraging them to *"go for it!"* Then one day someone said to me, "You ought to write a book, your story and ideas are so inspiring." The thought of writing, much less reading a book, broke me out in a sweat. After the fear subsided, I remembered what my core belief in life was and that it got me to where I am today. *If I truly believe in myself, with determination, I can do anything.* So I took on the challenge. Not only did I want to once again prove it to be true, but I wanted to use it as an inspiration to others, whether it was for other dyslexics like myself or for those who need a little encouragement.

Terri L. Bowersock

Terri's Story:
Turning A Disability
Into An Opportunity

quote

*"With determination
and belief in yourself,
you can do anything."*

Terri L. Bowersock

Believing
I Was Dumb

Big red pen marks scrawled across my papers saying "poor work" and "lazy" are perhaps my most vivid school memories.

While other second graders were starting to read, I was staring at the alphabet chart trying to figure out what the letters meant. By third grade, I was drowning in a sea of confusion. I kept making mistakes the others weren't making any longer. It seemed like all the other kids were learning and growing up, but I was stuck being dumb and still a baby. My parents also knew something was wrong, I think they thought I was retarded. So they took me to a specialist for testing.

The diagnosis was dyslexia. What's that? Definition: Most people think this learning disorder means seeing letters backward. What it actually means, however, is that dyslexics *recall* letters backward or out of place. The left side of our brain, the side that organizes letters and numbers in sequence, misfires when we try to recall how to spell a word, read a sentence or do math. Think of it as accessing a file on a computer and the document coming up scrambled and out of order.

What was I going to do with my new found label? Was I stupid? I started to avoid, at all costs, reading and writing. When I came face-to-face with having to read out loud, I turned into the class clown, hoping to be kicked out to the hallway. Once out in the hall, I slinked down to the floor and felt the tears flow. I wasn't a bad kid! I wasn't a trouble maker!

I hated spelling bees, never once passing my first turn. To pass a test, I had to cheat. I still remember my teacher yelling at me to "keep my eyes on my own paper, cheaters are "bad." I had a choice to make right then and there, either turn my paper in with nothing on it and look totally stupid or to get a lot better at cheating. I opted for cheating. If I hadn't, I'd be the oldest third grader in America!

Despite my improved cheating abilities, I still flunked third grade. It became quite clear to me. I needed more survival skills other than cheating to get through school.

Skill one: I learned that if the teacher liked me I had a better chance of passing—regardless of my grades. So I concentrated on getting them to like me.

Skill two: When other kids were making fun of me and calling me names, it was better to join in and make a joke, hiding my true feelings. As time went on, I even went a step further, and cut myself down first before anyone else could. I thought my emotions didn't count, buying into the concept that everyone was better than me.

Skill three: It was better to lay low and blend into the background. The less attention I drew to myself, the better. I stayed away from joining any clubs and never volunteered for any projects.

Moving through the educational process was emotionally debilitating. I'll never, ever forget in high school the day the SAT scores were posted in the cafeteria. Now it was clear for all to see that I was a *"dummy."* Not surprisingly, this academic status prevented me from fitting in with any of the accepted groups. Cheerleaders, band members, yearbook members, and newspaper staff clearly wanted nothing to do with a dummy.

As a result, I developed low self-esteem and found myself accepted only by the "bad kids" who hung out across the street. Even then, I knew I wasn't really a bad kid. I didn't like to break rules and somehow I managed to be somewhere else when the real trouble happened. Unfortunately, that can't be said for everyone in groups such as mine. In fact, statistics show that 80 percent of children in the juvenile prison system are documented as learning disabled.

Finally high school graduation came in 1975. I managed to get through a two-year community college program, thanks to most of my classes focusing on discussion groups rather than testing and writing assignments. Unfortunately, it was a different story at Arizona State University, where I lasted only two months.

School was over. It was time to enter the workforce and live on my own. But all I had was a third grade reading level and fifth grade math skills. How was I going to get a job when I couldn't even fill out a job application?

Taking A First Swing At Business

After considering my options, I decided my best bet was to start my own business—a lunch golf cart at a Phoenix resort where my mom worked as a tennis pro. Each morning at 11:30 a.m., I would sit out in the golf cart with an ice chest packed with pop and sandwiches that Mom helped me make that morning. That is where I learned how to sell. If you are going to interrupt a golfer, you had better have a darn good sales pitch!

Before long, Mom secured the concession for a gift shop at another resort. While she taught tennis, I managed the gift shop. This was an opportunity to use my sales abilities and talk, talk, talk. Most importantly, it was my chance to learn the retail business.

I'll never forget the day I learned to make a profit. I had gotten in a box of shoelaces for tennis shoes and added the shipping costs. I remember thinking, at this rate...I'm going to have to sell a lot of shoelaces to survive! But I had forgotten one thing: Profit! This is a lesson I have not forgotten since: cost + shipping + profit = the selling price.

Still, at the age of 21, I knew the income from this small shop would not be enough to support me forever. So, I set out to create a new and better future.

Creating that new and better future made me realize that I had to conquer all the negative leftovers from school days—the days of red pen marks and my fifth grade teacher, who told me I was "as dumb as a cue ball" while he used a yardstick as a pool cue to tap my head.

Determination And Discovery

I wanted to become "somebody." I needed to show my friends, family and teachers that I wasn't dumb; and I definitely wasn't lazy. I needed to prove myself and I needed to do it in a big way.

When I pictured my future, the word successful didn't fit. *Very successful, now that fit perfectly!* I didn't know exactly how I was going to achieve that status, but I knew I would.

The answer came during a trip to Kansas to see my father. While sitting on the plane I started thinking about my future. What future? I thought I would never be able to have a career. Tears filled my eyes and I prayed no one would start talking to me for fear I would burst out crying.

Once there, Dad took me to visit Betty, his friend who operated the Clearing House Consignment Shop out of a little house. There, I saw sterling silver, china, small furniture, and knick-knacks for sale. People were actually having fun as they purchased what others no longer needed or wanted!

Betty graciously explained how she managed the business. By the time the day was over, I knew I could do it. I knew I had the sales skills, and most importantly, I understood how the retail formula (cost + profit = price) applied to the consignment business.

My mind took off in a million directions as I visualized how my store would look. By midnight, I had my business and its launch all figured out. I jumped out of bed and called Mom to tell her about our next new adventure.

"We're going to be rich!" I said excitedly.

"Oh, now what?" she said in a sleepy voice. With great enthusiasm, I explained the whole idea.

She immediately responded, "You mean we are going to be like 'Sanford and Son?' We are going to haul junk and sell used furniture? I'm going back to sleep. I'll talk to you later." Mom was as unenthusiastic as I was enthusiastic.

On the flight home, I concentrated on a way to convince mom that a consignment store was our ticket to success. I drew up a business plan to show her what the store would look like. However, it wasn't a typical business plan. I created mine with crayons and colored pencils. Designing my success, I actually drew how the store would look. Although Mom wasn't totally convinced by my plan, my persuasiveness and determination to move forward, convinced her.

Immediately, my mind started racing as I saw my business being successful. I focused on my future, my dreams, and my goals, leaving behind the labels school had given me. I decided at that moment to listen to only one voice: Mine. What an energizing feeling to finally understand that *I was in charge of my own future!*

A Business Is Born

Mom and I borrowed $2,000 from my grandmother (the only loan I have ever taken while running my $26 million dollar business). With my newly developed determination, I set out to bring my vision to reality.

Climbing on my college-days' motorcycle, I went to find a store location. I was so naïve I didn't know there were real estate people willing to do this legwork! I saw a "For Lease" sign and went in to chat with the storeowner. After agreeing to the monthly rent, I was handed the lease to sign. Unable to read the legal jargon, I faked reading it. Carefully, I guessed how long it would take to read a document that size. After waiting for that amount of time to pass, and not a moment longer, I eagerly signed my name. Presto! I was in business!

I set up a bed in the back of the store and lived there to save housing expenses. On my first day, I opened the doors with only my childhood bedroom furniture and Mom's living room furniture as stock.

I will never forget those first few weeks. People would walk in and ask, "What is this place?" and I would excitedly explain that it was a consignment store. "Bring me what you want or need to sell and I'll sell it for you!" I said.

The first woman who took me up on my offer had a "hidden agenda." She had a storage room filled with papers and junk. My job was to clean out the storage room, toss the junk and move any useable furniture to my store for resale. Mom and I started loading up an old truck that our customer had borrowed. Holding one end of a table, I backed into the bed of the truck, which had rotted out. *Plunk*, my leg disappeared through a hole! I pulled my bloody, scraped leg from the hole and finished loading the table...after all, I had a store to fill.

Although experiences such as these didn't increase Mom's appreciation for our new business, she continued to help me while still teaching tennis. Before long, business was increasing and instead of borrowing other people's trucks, we needed our own. We found an old discolored blue truck at just the right price ... cheap! I climbed behind the wheel for a test drive. After locating an abandoned parking lot, I floored it and the truck picked up speed nicely. Then, I stomped on the brakes and we came to a screeching stop. Yep! The brakes work! Glancing over, Mom was too frozen with fear to say "no." So, we bought "Ol' Blue." "Wow," I thought, "Now we have our own trucking service!"

The Most Important Day Of My Career

Then came the turning point of my business career. I discovered that I had a talent that would prove to be one of the most valuable elements of building my small, one-store location into a national chain of consignment stores.

My store was located on a busy street where cars drove past at 50 miles an hour. Somehow I had to slow them down and draw attention to my business.

So we put furniture on the curb and propped up a mannequin from Mom's tennis shop. Dressed in a short tennis skirt and one of Mom's wigs, the mannequin appeared to be happily waving at people driving by. Truck drivers even honked and whistled as they drove by the store, not realizing that she was a mannequin. One day a truck went speeding by and with a big whoosh, she fell into the street and both of her arms were knocked off!

Seizing the opportunity, I called the newspaper. "There's been a mannequin accident!" I shouted. Before long, a reporter arrived.

"There's been a what?" he asked.

"There's been a mannequin accident! Over there!" I pointed.

Two days later, a big picture of our mannequin, broken arms and all, along with a story about Terri's Consignment Store appeared in the newspaper. If this had been an advertisement, it would have cost us $2,000!

I'd *finally* found something I was good at. I—*Terri, the dummy*—had a talent for promotion, marketing and advertising!

Getting In The Swing Of Business

That small article generated a great deal of interest. More and more furniture arrived. Mom and I also found new ways to get furniture for the store. While attending our first auction, packed in a very crowded room, we were separated. By the time the bidding started, I'd located a great piece and began bidding. The competition and the fast pace bidding was intense. Suddenly, the auctioneer who knew us, stopped the bidding, looked at me and then across the room at Mom.

"Are you two ladies together?" he asked. I pushed my way through the crowd and found myself looking into my mother's eyes.

"Yes sir," I responded.

"Well, you're bidding against each other!" he replied.

Boy, did we feel like amateurs! The auctioneer started the bidding over with just one of us bidding—this time not against each other. We did, however, get that piece and fifteen others. We loaded everything into "Ol' Blue" and drove home at the break neck speed of

15 miles per hour. Moving any faster would have caused us to lose our precious load. During the next few months, mom and I did bounce a few sofas and chairs from "Ol' Blue" until I had wood siding built around the truck bed. Then everything stayed in place. We were becoming professional movers. We even painted our company name on the side of the truck—just like the big stores did!

Getting consignment furniture was just one piece of the puzzle. Making our consigned items attractive to buyers was another piece. One day, I visited an acquaintance's home and was impressed by his decorating abilities. Later, he came down to the store and commented that the store would be much more appealing if the furniture were arranged in room settings. Like a fairy godfather, he returned for several days and magically made the store look like a design studio.

Furniture began selling faster in complete room settings with our new look. Needing more help to get it all delivered, I used my persuasion skills once again on Mom. How could I convince her to leave the tennis business and work with me full time? I simply pointed out Arizona's high rate of skin cancer. It worked! I convinced her to give up teaching tennis and take up the consignment business full time.

Eight months later, the lease I had pretended to read turned out to be an illegal sublease. Along came the real building owner, who gave us 30 days to move or have the doors locked. Everything I owned and everything that was consigned would be trapped inside! Once again, I was on the street looking for a home for Terri's Consignment Store—I had learned my first legal lesson. It is cheaper to have a lawyer read legal documents before signing them than to pay the consequences.

Using the opportunity to expand our business, we rented a 3,000-sq. ft. space for our second location. Hidden behind a big warehouse without street exposure to bring in customers for us, this new location made one thing clear. It was again time to find another story for the media to create publicity.

It was the early 1980s and Arizona had one of the nation's highest divorce rates. That was it! I called a local newspaper reporter and told her the story of a divorced mother and her daughter who were running their own business. This was especially newsworthy, given that such stories were usually about father-and-son businesses. The result was a front-page picture and feature article in the Sunday edition of *The Phoenix Gazette* with more pictures on the inside. The next day, 300 people, mostly mothers and daughters came to the store. In addition to helping boost our monthly sales volume from $40,000 to $60,000, the article set off a series of stories in small neighborhood newspapers and several magazines.

The article also launched a new direction for Terri's Consignment Store. Known for having quality *"gently-used"* furniture at great prices, the store became a regular source for professional interior designers. Mom began to order some new items, so that we could consistently provide both the new and *"gently-used"* furnishings that designers wanted. Proud of the new concept we had created, Terri's Consignment Furniture then became Terri's Consign & Design. Thanks to Mom, we were no longer "Sanford and Son."

My next marketing effort set the company in its own pioneering category. No one had ever seen a television commercial for used furniture. Used cars, yes, but not furniture. I told Mom about the idea. She said, "No, it costs too much." Determined to be the first consignment store to advertise on television, I secretly saved the money needed and arranged for a production crew—without telling her until the day before the filming.

As the cameramen tried to shoot the commercial, Mom frantically scurried around dusting the store.

At the end of the spot, he told her to hand me the feather duster.

"Thanks, Mom," I sarcastically replied, like any typical daughter.

"Thanks, Mom," became the signoff of many TV commercials to come over the next ten years. Those two words established us as a mother-daughter business to the moms, step-moms and grandmothers who make the majority of furniture purchases. For years, mothers visiting the store would pinch my cheeks and say, "What a sweet daughter you are." Boy, did I have rosy cheeks! But our bank account was doubling, so I didn't mind.

Goodbye, Mom
And Taking The Next Step

Mom and I worked side-by-side every day for eight years. Together, we picked up furniture in the morning, sold it all day and delivered it after we closed the store at night.

I will never forget delivering a sofa to a third floor apartment one evening. Mom came down the stairs on swollen feet with her hand on her aching back.

"I'd rather have skin cancer!" she grumbled, recalling my sales pitch that took her from the tennis court to the consignment business.

The consignment business had worn her out. Knowing I could not stand in her way, I bought out Mom's half-interest in the business. As she went on to pursue a less physically demanding job of selling real estate; I pursued my dream of building the nationwide chain of stores I'd drawn in my colored-pencil business plan.

With the realization that I needed better reading and writing skills to run the business on my own, I contacted a professor specializing in learning disabilities at the University of Arizona. Frustrated after weeks of trying to learn what seemed like inconsistent and unorganized rules for grammer, I gave up. At that point, I asked the teacher to give me the rules for each vowel and consonant one at a time. In four months I invented a simplified visual mapping method for spelling. With the help of a friend, these spelling maps are now part of a self-published workbook sold at conferences on learning disabilities. Who would have thought that the girl who cheated on spelling tests would develop a new method for learning phonics? This method, by the way, took my spelling from the third to the eighth grade level and my reading from third grade to college level. From my new ability to read, I found out there were famous people who were dyslexic including Walt Disney and Albert Einstein. It gave me a sense of belonging and hope.

(You will find a list of famous people with learning disabilities listed in the appendix of this book.)

Armed with my improved skills, I opened four Terri's Consign & Design stores during the next three years. Now I needed another public relations story to spread the word and keep growing. It was at this time that former First Lady Barbara Bush was starting the Literacy Volunteer Program. (One of her sons also happens to be dyslexic.) Breaking with my tradition of hiding my dyslexia, I once again called the reporters. Only this time, it was television news reporters. Setting off a chain reaction, I was on the noon, three, and five o'clock news broadcasts. From that exposure, the United States Chamber of Commerce and Connecticut Mutual Life Insurance nominated me for the Blue Chip Award, given to small businesses for their resourcefulness, resilience and determination. In a matter of weeks, my story was being told in national magazines.

Taking The Company National

Armed with growing exposure, I was ready to fulfill my dream of opening stores from coast-to-coast. Making that happen meant franchising and I turned to several consultants for assistance. The first promised a pot of gold and he was the only one to find it. He got $80,000 and I learned to spell the word f-r-a-n-c-h-i-s-e!

Eventually, I learned enough to put the right plan together. The first person interested in buying a franchise was a businessperson that just so happened to have a background in franchising. Rather than sell Marcus Curtis a franchise, I again used my persuasion skills and convinced him to join my second enterprise…Terri's Consign & Design Franchise, Inc. Several other key people—Chief Executive Officer, Kevin Crippa and Chief Operating Officer, Shelley Santucci—joined the business as well. Each of these people has provided the vital experience and knowledge needed to make our business a success.

In the meantime, I had won *Inc. Magazine's* 1992 Retail Entrepreneur of the Year award. Newspaper stories generated interest in my franchises. As my first franchise owner signed on the bottom line, he told me he was dyslexic. "If you can do it, so can I," he said. He was right. Within just eight months, he and his wife made back their original investment and were drawing a good salary. They opened their second store within two years. Soon, there were four more franchise owners.

To further the company's exposure, I took a personal interest in public speaking. I started speaking for free at schools and prisons, for women's groups, Rotary Clubs—you name it, I did it! All the while, I knew that the experience was helping me build confidence to speak professionally.

As a result of public speaking on learning disabilities and involvement with the International Disabilities Association and other organizations, *Inc. Magazine* nominated me in 1994 for a second honor, the Socially Responsible Entrepreneur Award. This brought exposure in other national magazines, including *Entrepreneur Magazine*. It also brought growing interest in Terri's Consign & Design. Our customer base continued to grow and even included celebrities such as Kenny Rogers, the Beach Boys, Alice Cooper, Willy Mays, Hugh Downs, Walter Cronkite and Geordie Hormel. We added two more Phoenix locations and in 1997 opened the Atlanta, Georgia market, which is set to become the eastern hub for Terri's Consign & Design.

My Dreams Came True With Oprah

The company's growth, increased exposure and additional awards continued with a snowball effect. In 1998, I won the Avon Woman of Enterprise Award—one I had tried to win earlier and thankfully had not given up on. This award, one I am very honored to have received, brought perhaps the most exciting phone call of my life. My receptionist, Sarah, answered the incoming call.

"Hi, this is Ray with the 'Oprah Winfrey Show,'" said the voice on the other end.

"Yeah right," Sarah responded.

"Why do people always say that?" Ray said with a chuckle.

Convinced it really was the "Oprah Show," Sarah came to me and said, "The 'Oprah Show' is on the line."

I started to say "yeah right" but before I could get it out, Sarah jumped in with, "Don't, I already said that, and believe it or not, it really is the 'Oprah Show.'"

The night before the show, I sat outside on my patio looking at the night sky while enjoying a beautiful desert spring evening. It suddenly hit me: I had made it! It wasn't just about making money or that I had built a company that stretched from coast to coast. It was about healing an old wound. My appearance on Oprah was going to let me do what I wanted to do years ago. I was going to stand up in front of the world and proclaim, "See, I'm not stupid. I'm not lazy. I made it! I am a success." Better yet, I wasn't going to say it, Oprah was.

I am really thankful to Oprah. Being on her show taught me that you have to know what drives your own success. When that day came, I stopped, took a deep breath and really felt it for the first time. It wasn't about proving to others that I was smart...I had to know it for myself. Since then, I have had a sense of peace, not trying to run so hard and prove so much.

Planning For The Future

Today, Terri's Consign & Design Furnishings, Inc. and Terri's Consign & Design Franchise are positioned to grow in other areas. Together with my key team members, we've opened Art Upholstery, and Terri-K's Investment Corp., a real estate company.

As this chapter ends, another story begins with the start of a fifth company, Terri's Publishing & Speaking. This new business allows me to share my story and message with others. That message is, quite simply: *believe in yourself and never give up!* I couldn't read or spell, so I developed other skills that have taken me far beyond the limitations of my disability. Can you imagine a dyslexic writing a book?

2

Live Your Dreams Today With Determination

quote

"When you know what you want to achieve and value the lesson that gives you your drive in life, determination is the vehicle to your success."

Terri L. Bowersock

Why Read Another Book?

Why are you attending another inspirational seminar or reading another motivational book?

If you are asking yourself that question, the answer is simple. You have a dream. You keep chasing it around in your mind. But you need a little additional encouragement to make it your reality. Maybe you just need inspiration to make your dream bigger and better. Inside, a little voice keeps pushing. You know that you have to continue searching until you find that one *"thing"* that moves you to finally take a risk. The challenge is discovering what that *"thing"* is that will drive you to succeed.

Motivation is like a fingerprint—individualized to each person. One of my favorite examples is my "weight story." I had gained a lot of weight and tried everything known to man to lose the extra pounds. I tried the "soup diet" and bought oils to rub on my feet. I ordered exercise machines that looked like easy fixes from infomercials. I even tried acupuncture on my ears. Nothing worked for very long. I would lose some weight and then seemingly overnight the pounds were back. I was exhausted and discouraged.

One evening a friend, who also had a weight problem, walked into a party I was attending. I didn't even recognize her. She had lost 40 pounds in four months! I knew I had finally found it. I had found the *"thing"* (in this case, a person) that would inspire me to reach my goal.

My friend had tried as many crazy ideas as I had to lose weight. I figured, if she could do it; I could do it! I invited her to my house and together we cleaned out my refrigerator, removing any future temptations. She took the time to explain how she reached her goal. Her success and enthusiasm motivated me to try the *Dr. Atkins Diet*. I lost ten pounds in the first two weeks and along the way changed my lifestyle. I began eating healthier and including mild exercise in my daily routine. The most important part is that I found my motivation and with my mentor, I could continue on my path to successful weight loss.

Was it easy? No. Changing a behavior pattern is always difficult. However, it brings great rewards. In my case, it has brought pride in reaching my goal, an improved my self-image.

What Is Your Determination?

How do you find your motivation? First, remain open to new ideas. Always look for the key to your determination. Keep reading, attending seminars, listening to tapes and watching videos. Do whatever it takes to find that one *"thing"* that motivates you to reach your goal.

Because of my dyslexia, my determination was the need to prove to myself, family and friends that I was smart. After years of embarrassment and hiding my disability, I discovered that we all have some kind of disability. It can be fear, an addiction, an illness, or a physical handicap. Other examples of disabilities could be an emotional or economic disadvantage or even as simple as something you don't like about yourself.

How can a disability become a motivator? Understand your particular disability and use it instead of hating it. Value the lessons it has triggered for you. Let yourself respect and cherish the gifts it brings to you. Use the experience to fuel the fire that will drive you to your success!

You may have heard it said that anyone who has suffered through a disability, critical illness, death, abuse, or addiction knows the courage it takes to heal. The insight from these transforming experiences gives you hope and teaches you that the reward for courage is wisdom. With wisdom comes the determination to make changes in your life.

Until I was 30, I cursed my disability and felt dyslexia was what held me back and proved that I wasn't as smart as everyone else. Then one day life's lessons finally taught me that who I am today and my determination to succeed was because of my disability.

Favorite Stories Of Determination

Ron Popiel

Ron Popiel, who has grossed more than $300 million with his inventions including the Veg-O-Matic and the Pocket Fisherman, explained in his book, *The Salesman of the Century*, the major difference between those who achieve success and those who do not. He pointed out that successful people keep working and trying until they reach their goal while unsuccessful people contemplate and discuss ideas but don't take action.

Mary Kay

In 1963, Mary Kay became widowed while in her 50s. Unable to obtain a bank loan, she started her cosmetics firm with $5,000. Today, her firm remains the world's second largest direct sales cosmetics company. You are never too old to start your dream.

Dave Thomas

An adopted child who dropped out of high school, Thomas is founder and chairman of Wendy's International, a $6 billion dollar company. He knew he wanted to work in the restaurant business and felt he could learn more by working than schooling. In his book, *Well Done*, Thomas noted that while quitting school made the business world tougher, he learned that anything was possible with hard work.

Paul J. Orfalea

The founder of Kinko's, which now has more than 500 copy centers across the country, Orfalea flunked second grade and struggled as a non-reader. He was expelled from seven different schools before finally graduating from high school. While in college, he filled a void by providing a campus copy center and then went on to develop centers on other campuses.

Oprah Winfrey

Born a poor, African-American, illegitimate female in rural Mississippi, Winfrey has gone from a local news anchor to a media star who is worth millions and has a tremendous influence on adults. Oprah says her mission is for "people to have the grandest vision for their lives."

While on her show, she showed me that anyone could truly run a company with the spirit of love. In her presence, as well as that of her employees, I could feel the spirit of love.

Success
Through Thinking
And Visualization

quote

*"What you think every day,
every minute, every second,
is what you are tomorrow."*

Terri L. Bowersock

Your Life Is An Expression Of Your Mind

As human beings, we are free to will whatever we desire through the use of our thoughts and words. I know what you are thinking, "Yeah sure, I can change the world by thinking about it." But take a minute and consider this fact—*thoughts produce actions*.

Undeniably, the one thing you have absolute control over is your attitude, which is nothing more than your thoughts and words. When you approach life with a positive, optimistic outlook, you create an environment reflecting that attitude. Have you ever noticed that when you are in a particularly happy or enthusiastic mood, everyone around you seems to be experiencing the same mood? It's not by accident! What you think and feel has a tremendous effect on others because our lives our linked to the world around us.

Experiment with this idea by beginning your day with a positive approach. During every interaction with others, consciously think positive thoughts about the other person and about the situation being discussed. You will be absolutely amazed at the power you have to determine the emotional atmosphere in your immediate environment.

I know for myself, before going into a meeting, I set the mood with enthusiastic energy. It always amazes me how well the meeting turns out.

Knowing that you have this power is the key to changing your life. Desiring change—whether it is for health, financial, personal or career reasons—requires you *to change your thinking!*

If positive thinking has positive results, then what happens when you think negative thoughts? You make yourself—and most likely those around you—miserable.

Consider those "bad days" when it seems that absolutely nothing else could go wrong. Then suddenly, it does. Congratulations! All those "terrible little thoughts" you have allowed to run amuck in your mind just proved how right you are. Isn't the human mind marvelous? It does exactly what you tell it!

Think of this sequence of events as the "ripple" effect. When you drop a stone in water, you can watch the little rings grow into great big rings. The same thing happens with negative thoughts. When you focus on a "little bad thing" that has happened, you can watch it grow into a "big bad thing." Why does this happen? Because most people do not realize the power that their "little thoughts" have. With effort, you can change your thinking and thereby produce the most awesome changes in your life. Remember: *the power you have within your mind is limitless.*

Defend Yourself With Positive Thinking

Let's take it further. If your thoughts affect you and others, then their thoughts affect you, right? You bet they do! But you are not at their mercy. You can defend yourself against the negative thoughts of others.

How? Start by thinking positive, caring and loving things about yourself. Most of us have spent the better part of our lives being told to watch our egos and not be "full" of ourselves. There is a huge difference between being a self-confident individual and being arrogant. Self-confidence is good! Encourage it and watch it grow!

When you first begin practicing this defense method, it may be easier for you to close your eyes and concentrate on a time when you felt cared for, loved or appreciated. With practice, you will learn to radiate positive thoughts about yourself without anyone near you knowing this. If you stay positive and loving, negative thoughts cannot create a weakness in your life. Go ahead; have some fun. Practice this with your family and friends. Think positive and stay strong!

Visualization With Affirmations

Part of positive thinking is to have affirmations or statements that you say over and over to yourself. However, to imprint your positive thoughts in your mind and ultimately have them result in positive actions, you must add visualization. This means not only thinking and saying positive thoughts, but also using your senses.

Research shows that you retain ten percent of what you read. When you read something and actually see it or picture it in your mind, you retain 55 percent. However, when you read something, see or picture it, *plus* have an emotional response attached to it, your retention climbs to a full 100 percent! Using all three—reading, visualizing and feeling—

overlays the current images in your subconscious with a predetermined outcome in the form of new images and emotions.

Let's say your goal is to have a red Jaguar. You think positive thoughts about it and say to yourself, "I know I can be successful and have a red Jaguar." You read a brochure describing the car's features and picture yourself driving the sleek red Jag in your mind. Next, you feel the wind in your hair as you drive with the top down. You pull up to the stoplight and the driver in the lane beside you looks over your new car with an approving smile. You are proud of your success and its rewards as you effortlessly pull away from the light.

When you add visualizations such as these to your affirmations, you are using your brain's full power. As a result, your affirmations and positive thinking will be stronger...and the changes in your life more amazing!

When I think about a new idea or an image of what I want to do, I say it to myself. Then I envision how it will look. Next, I add a feeling to the idea. For example, when I first thought of building a successful business, I told myself I wanted to go to my class reunion in a limousine. I pictured driving up in a big, long beautiful car. I felt proud as friends and teachers realized I was a successful. More importantly, I replaced the negative idea that my friends and teachers thought I was dumb with these positive thoughts, images and feelings.

When I decided to become a national speaker, I chanted affirmations in my mind and felt the feeling of helping others, especially other learning disabled people. I envisioned the looks on their faces and the sparkle in their eyes as they too realized and believed that they could be successful too. Write it, see it, feel it, and it is yours.

Understand The Power Of Thinking

What is the most important difference between a successful and an unsuccessful person? Successful people understand that their mind has the power to determine their future. They do not allow their thoughts to control them. Instead, they control their thoughts.

People frequently say to me, "I bet you never thought your business would get so big because you are a woman." According to today's society and stereotypes, I should timidly reply that my success was a surprise to me. The truth is, however, that from my first crayon business plan, I always knew that my business would get big. And it's going to get bigger!

How do I know? Because from the very start, I have always envisioned a chain of stores. In my mind, I have actually seen people coming in and having a great time as they find treasures at Terri's Consign & Design. I have visualized how each store would look and what would happen during each TV commercial. I have never let myself doubt my thoughts or imagination. In short, I have simply believed that I can do anything I set my mind to do.

Now, think positive, visualize your dream, and know that you can create your success. Decide for yourself. Are you in control or are your thoughts?

Things That Can Destroy Your Success

Too often, people leave their minds open to negative influences. Here are some things that can destroy your success:

1. Lack of a clear picture of goals and a well-defined purpose in life.

2. Poor self control. You must have self-discipline.

3. An unhealthy body. Negative thoughts poison our bodies.

4. Overeating foods you know are bad for your health.

5. Overindulging in smoking, alcohol or drugs.

6. Lack of proper physical exercise.

7. Procrastinating or waiting for the right time. Remember, that you can start today with just a baby step.

8. Giving up.

9. Falling for the "get rich quick" plan or the gambling instinct.

10. Over or under-spending. Buying to show off or buying beyond your means can lead to failure. Being too thrifty because you fear poverty can result in missed opportunities.

11. Prejudice. Despite different religions, races, political beliefs, genders, sexual orientation or disabilities, we are all human beings.

12. Dishonesty. Be honest with employees, customers and most importantly yourself.

Some Successful Positive Thinkers

Thomas A. Edison

Others tried to convince this man who had only three
months of formal education, that he could not build a
machine that would record the human voice. Edison
knew that the mind could produce anything it could
conceive and believe. As a result, today we enjoy
recorded music, information and more.

F.W. Woolworth

This man was told that he would go broke trying to
run a five and dime store. Woolworth knew he could
be successful and backed his plans with faith and
determination. As a result, the term "dime store"
became part of the English language.

Henry Ford

"I'll belt the earth with dependable motor cars," this
positive thinker proclaimed to the world. Few people
believed Ford's sixth grade education could take him

to the top financially, but Ford himself believed. Today, not a moment passes without the world seeing the results of his belief.

Remember, with determination and positive thinking, you can do anything!

Sample Affirmations

Change them, create your own or use them just as they are. Don't forget to believe them. Incorporate them in your daily thoughts and above all, feel them.

Management Affirmations:

- We are experts at delegating responsibilities and seeing our people experience the victory of results.

- We influence the environment to help create tremendous growth in our people.

- We believe, understand, and practice total accountability.

- We are receiving tremendous gratification from 100 percent customer satisfaction.

- We are excited about accomplishing a $_____ profit.

- We are tremendously proud of the professional, happy and productive employees we lead.

- We love the pleasant, smooth running operation we maintain.

Employee Affirmations:

- I treat all customers like they are my only customer.

- Everyone I talk to is a buyer.

- I am a super salesperson and grow every day in every way.

- I keep abreast of current information and can cope with any challenge that arises.

- I bring out the best in all my customers by quickly discovering their specific needs.

- It is fun and easy to be organized.

Personal Affirmations:

- I like and respect myself.

- I know I am a worthy, capable and a valuable person.

- I show that I'm 100 percent alive by thinking, acting, and speaking with great enthusiasm.

- I have a positive expectation of winning big and I take temporary setbacks easily.

- I look for ways to encourage myself and others.

- I am very effective and efficient in stressful situations.

- I guide my own destiny and I am accountable for the results of my decisions and actions.

- I reinforce my successes and correct my errors.

- I am warm and friendly with everyone I come in contact with.

- I treat everyone with consideration and respect.

■ I have an exciting life with exciting people around me.

■ I quietly do helpful and worthwhile things for others.

■ I help my family members in any way I can.

■ I have an excellent free flowing memory with clear and easy recall.

■ I enjoy taking calculated risks to improve.

■ I am healthy and full of love, life and energy.

■ I love myself, including my emotions, mind, and body.

■ By loving myself more, I can love others more.

■ I have happy, fulfilling relationships.

■ I enjoy my work and its financial and personal rewards.

■ I will easily have the things I need, including love and money.

■ I am creating happiness in all aspects of my life.

■ I understand the purpose of my life.

■ I am happily challenged and creatively fulfilled.

How You Can
Design Your
Own Success

quote

"It takes many different ways of thinking to succeed. But it's how well you tie them all together that rockets you to the highest you can possibly imagine."

Terri L. Bowersock

What You Have To Do To Be Successful

Balance; don't burn out

It's not uncommon to hear that successful people are often workaholics. For example, Sam Walton, founder of Wal-Mart, said he often started at 4:30 a.m. and worked Saturdays to get a jump on the next week. When I first heard that, I seriously questioned myself, "Does it take sacrifice to be successful?" It was not appealing to me to forfeit my personal life day after day for a successful work life. It took a few years and some hard lessons for the answer to surface, "I didn't have to sacrifice."

To have a balanced life requires three different types of work: *focused work, teamwork* and *smart work.* Focused work is knowing what your goal is and not allowing yourself to stray from it. Teamwork happens when you trust others to take some of the load, whether it's outside sources, employees or volunteers. At home, success comes much easier with the support from everyone in the family. No one needs to do all the work maintaining the house or bear all the responsibility of raising the children. It takes a team. Smart work is knowing how to be a true leader. A good leader hires people smarter than themselves for the betterment of the company. My energy is put to use best by supporting and motivating my team to do their best and to grow in their own abilities.

To sum it up: work focused, then build a team so there can be growth, then lead for the future. Do not try to be all and do all.

Recognize the importance of nurturing

Our world needs the balanced energy of both males and females. Women as well as men play a role in politics, medicine, land development, human rights, animal rights and more. Our unique ability to nurture is vital not only to the existence of our planet but also to making it a better place to live.

Nurturing abilities also play a key role in the business world. Think what a difference a caring and kind nature can make to the thousands and thousands of unhappy, unmotivated and unappreciated employees trapped in today's companies.

One of the many ways I nurture my employees is to help them feel good about themselves. Our performance evaluation forms are not constructed as is typical: excellent worker, fair worker or poor worker. Instead they are rated: exceeds job performance, acceptable job performance, or does not meet the requirements of the job. That way their self-esteem is not graded by their job. We are talking about employee performance in their job, not rating them as a person.

Stop and imagine how wonderful it would be to live and work in a caring world. We all play a vital and valuable role in making such a world become a reality.

All things are important

A friend of mine owns a llama ranch and she told me about a lady who came to visit. The llamas would always spit at her. She said "Why do they always just spit on me and no one else?"

My friend said, "Because you think you are better than they are. For example, do you think you are more important than the leaves on a tree?"

"Of course, I'm human, they're not."

My friend humbly replied, "Without leaves giving oxygen, you would not breathe. When you think the llama is equal to you, they will stop spitting."

She processed this thought and on her next visit she remained dry.

I practice this strongly in my life. Never judge, for we are all here learning our own lessons. I understand that I am only one piece of the puzzle. No bigger, no smaller.

People have asked me, "How do you practice bringing spiritual consciousness to work?"

I answer, "Years ago I used to play a game with myself. I would imagine an enlightened being would join me for a day (for me it was Jesus, but for you it might be Gandhi, Buddha, Mother Theresa, or another). Knowing Jesus was by my side, I would walk through the company greeting my employees more consciously and more lovingly. Not only would I say 'Good morning,' but I would really feel it. I would always find myself giving a little more, maybe by taking time to listen or showing a personal interest in an employee. When I would visit the stores I would reach out to the customers with a gentle touch. My idea was to experience total love of myself and mankind. After this I felt the joy of compassion. It took me to a level of true happiness and the rest of the day reflected this happiness not only in myself but in every one around me.

Eight Steps To Designing Success

1. Get rid of old fears.

The first step is to think back to your family or childhood. Are there negative thoughts or fears you may have picked up about success, money, racism or sexual stereotypes? Were you told that you'd never amount to anything or that you couldn't do anything right? Or, that all girls must be housewives and that boys must be the bread winners? Write all these negative thoughts down, then burn them and bury the ashes in the ground. There! Now they're dead! And you can be more alive than ever because you can replace those negative thoughts with positive ones that will take you where you want to be.

2. Know your dream and visualize it every day.

Live, think and breathe your dream every day. Make it part of you. Think of yourself as a walking projector. When you visualize your dream, it will play out in your words and actions and create a real-life movie about you accomplishing your goal.

What you think every day, every minute, every second, is what you are tomorrow. Simply put: visualize your dream today and it will become your reality tomorrow.

3. Gather information.

Know what you want to be and do, then get the specialized knowledge that you'll need to succeed.

An important consideration is to make sure that what you want to do is a sound, well thought out idea. You may want to open a video store, but with big national chains now dominating that industry, success may be hard to attain.

How do you know what is a good idea? A good idea is a product or service that people want and are willing to buy. It can be an exciting new twist on an old idea. Furniture certainly was not anything new when I started building Terri's Consign & Design in the early 1980s. But at that time, consignment stores did not even exist.

Southwest Airlines is another example of this concept. The airline was started by two businessmen who created a business plan on a napkin. Their idea was to make flying as cheap as driving. You know what that meant; in place of free dinners and beverages, passengers got low fares, 13 peanuts and a Coke.

Once you clearly know what you want to do, learn everything you can about your dream. Use the tools that work best for you: audio tapes, reading, travel or talking with people experienced in the area you are pursuing.

To create a nationwide chain of consignment stores, I set out to learn everything I could about furniture operations. I ordered every single entrepreneur workbook I could find. I researched used furniture and new furniture stores, instinctively knowing that I had to understand my competition and what made my store different in order to get to the top. For years, I measured the nationwide growth of consignment furniture by studying the *Yellow Page* directories at the local library.

I also became the "roads scholar" of the consignment industry. I literally went on the road and visited consignment stores across America. As a result, I got ideas and learned what worked and what didn't. By the time I was in business 12 years, my expertise was so well established that I became known as "The Consignment Guru."

4. Design your business plan.

Write down what you are going to do, how you are going to do it, how much money you need, the date this will be achieved, and a fixed number representing how much you are going to make, sell or produce and by when.

Writing your plan or mapping it in pictures will help you see it every day. It will also help you accomplish your goals. In fact, research has shown that people are 85 percent more likely to complete tasks that have been written down compared to tasks that haven't been put to paper.

Think of this plan as your "To Do List." That "To Do List" applies whether it is for weekly work or becoming a national success.

5. Take the risk today.

Beginning today, take the risk of making your dream come true, even if it's just a little step. Every day, do something to get one step closer to your dream.

For instance, once the decision was made to franchise Terri's Consign & Design, I moved forward in baby steps. My first venture was to mentor a woman from Prescott, Arizona. I shared my experience and knowledge of consignment furniture with her for the bargain fee of $800. Next came a gentleman from Washington, D.C. and a fee of $2,000. I continued to do consulting over the next few years and in the process learned how to be a franchisor. To date, we have seven successful franchises in operation and several more in the planning stages.

One of my other dreams was to be a national speaker. I wanted to speak to audiences about overcoming disabilities and achieving success. This came about after I won the Entrepreneur of the Year Award given by *Inc. Magazine* and was asked to deliver my first public speech.

Prior to the acceptance speech, I was nervous and even a little fearful. Could my simple ideas about success affect others? I didn't think I knew how to inspire people, but found out I did. The audience reaction was so overwhelming that I set out to share my story with everyone who wanted to listen.

I began creating the dream of being a national speaker. I pictured myself traveling the world to speak to audiences. To make my dream come true, I followed the same steps I used to create Terri's Consignment. I researched other speakers and learned from their experiences. I practiced writing and giving speeches. Then I just did it! I started speaking for free to schools and prisons, for women's groups, Rotary Clubs and others.

After each speaking engagement, people would gather around me and want to discuss how my speech had been helpful to them. I knew it was time to graduate from practice to profit. A real springboard was winning the 1998 Avon Woman of Enterprise Award, which resulted in an appearance on the "Oprah Winfrey Show." As the post-Oprah calls began rolling in with requests to speak nationally, I realized that my dream of being a paid national speaker had become reality.

No matter what you want to be—if it is a designer, start designing your friend's home for a small fee or no cost; if it is an actor, get involved in a community or church play—whatever it is, the best day to start doing it is today.

6. Don't let failure stop you.

Never, never, never give up. Your failures are the stepping stones to success. I learned my business by making mistakes, so did many successful people. Keep in mind that Mr. Hershey bankrupted three companies before he learned enough to succeed. Thomas Edison tried 2,000 times to invent the light bulb. He could have stopped at 1,999. Thankfully, he did not. Even Walt Disney was fired from a newspaper for lack of ideas!

7. Let a healthy body and mind enhance your leadership.

A healthy body that is well-exercised and not burdened with addictions will be strong and able to build your success. A healthy mind balances your emotions, your play time, your family time and work time. This brings the ability to become a great leader.

Develop your leadership skills. Know that you can do anything you put your mind to doing. Leadership is not the power to control people. It is setting good examples and sharing your enthusiasm so that fellow employees or family members feel proud to be a part of your business or family. They will feel like they are part of the team and that equals success for all.

8. Use the power of positive thinking.

Time and time again, it has been shown that positive thinking affects your energy and self-esteem. Likewise, thinking negative thoughts about yourself can undermine not only your self-esteem, but your future success. The good news is, thinking positive thoughts truly has the power to make incredibly awesome changes in your life.

Consider for a moment that thoughts are actually things that can be measured. Our thoughts travel at the speed of light, an amazing 186,000 miles per second which has been documented with a sound wave meter.

These thoughts and eight steps are what have made me successful. Above all, you will find success when you use them to guide your professional and your personal life. Start using them today and see for yourself!

The Bottom Line: Achieving Financial Success

quote

"If you become a millionaire just to count the cash, you'll never be rich."

Terri L. Bowersock

Know What Financial Success Is For You

Before you can achieve financial success, you must first have your own clear definition of what it means to be financially successful.

You can create the definition by asking yourself several questions. Do you want to start your own business? Do you want to work for someone else and work your way up in terms of income? How big of a house do you want and what will it cost? How much do you want for tithing, charity or supporting family members? How much do you want now? In five years? In 20 years? At retirement? How do you define financial success? Define what it is for you.

For me, creating and understanding my definition of financial success meant setting goals and priorities. I realized during this process that we are all entrepreneurs. I am responsible for myself, and you are responsible for yourself. Whether you own your own business or work for someone else, you still get up and go to work to earn money. If you are a business owner and grow in your abilities, you will increase the size and likely, the profitability of your business. If you are an employee and grow in your abilities, you will increase your income. If you are unhappy about your work, you change the circumstances or change jobs. When you understand that you are in control of your life and career and when you realize that your financial wealth depends on how you apply yourself—this is what makes you an entrepreneur. Whether you work for your own company or someone else's company, you are ultimately working for yourself.

I started my own company because I allowed myself to be guided by my higher self and I stayed open to the magic of life. I believed in myself and did not give up. My definition of financial success was owning a big home and filling it with beautiful furniture and art. I wanted to have plenty of wealth to enjoy my life, travel and learn about history. For me personally, making a million dollars—becoming a millionaire by age 40— was success.

With this in mind, I created a plan to achieve my goal. The first step was to invest in my business and keep reinvesting until it became a solid company.

The second step was to buy my dream home. (It is important to reward yourself along the way for your hard work!) The third step was to build a strong savings and investment portfolio to secure my retirement.

The fourth step was treating myself to life's toys and luxuries, such as fun cars, boats and travel. In addition to these items, I rewarded myself with smaller things along the road to success. Importantly, however, I did not buy things that I could not afford. I disciplined myself to spend wisely so that I could reinvest and reach my goal of becoming a millionaire by 1998. Thanks to this discipline, I have exceeded my goal many times over.

Remember, it's having a clear goal and the discipline to stick with your plan for achieving it.

Steps To Becoming A Millionaire

1. Believe you can be a millionaire.

In America, regardless of your race, sex or disability, you can be a millionaire. According to statistics, the typical American millionaire is an ordinary person who has achieved wealth and success over time. How? By working, planning and saving for it. America is the land of opportunity.

2. Make sure you enjoy the journey, not just the destination.

Have a healthy view of money. There are many stories of success. But all too often, they end with a rich person who dies lonely and without truly enjoying life. Let money be a part of your life, but not all of your life.

I've asked myself—if I saved and scrimped until I had a million dollars in my check book and on that day the monetary value of the dollar drops to a penny, would I have enjoyed the journey?

3. Understand money.

First you need to respect it; then master it; then grow it; then let it flow.

Respecting money means understanding that it is a very powerful tool for caring for your needs. On the other hand, it is not a tool for improving your self-image, controlling others, or making people like you. As a rule of thumb, anytime money is replacing an emotion, it is probably being used in the wrong way.

Mastering money means knowing how much you need and not letting it become a burden of debt. Today, there are many ways to get credit cards and money. But only you can be the controller of your money. From the very beginning, I had a mind set that I only spent what I had, nothing more.

Growing money means knowing how much you need to live on and what you have to invest or save. Set an amount that you want to earn by a certain age. Write this amount and this goal down. Keep visualizing it, saying it, and knowing it until you get there.

This may seem as if all you have to do is write your goal, say it a certain number of times daily, and presto, you will achieve it. What is really happening, however, is that this process requires you to set goals, become comfortable with having a certain amount, and motivate yourself to plan a way to achieve your goal.

Letting money flow means sharing with charities and others. Develop your ability to give by visualizing money coming in easily and flowing out easily to others. Know the percentage of your income that you want to tithe. Trust that it will be replenished for the greater good of man.

Achieving financial success does not come easy. But it does not have to come hard, either. Keep in mind that when you say negative statements such as "I don't have enough to pay bills," you are making it harder to manifest your future.

4. Love your work.

What you do makes the difference. When you truly love your work, you will devote your energy to your projects. The joy of building your business or creating your job will bring you success. Set your goals, pace yourself, and always increase your knowledge. As Henry Ford said, "If money is your hope for independence, you will never have it. The only real security that a person has is a reserve of knowledge, experience and ability."

5. Appoint yourself Chief Executive Officer (CEO).

Everyone is really self-employed, no matter who they work for. You hold the keys to your financial success. The key point is that you and you alone are in charge of your own destiny. When you are self-empowered, you always have choices. You can stay, move to another company, or make changes. For instance, my marketing director could have been on salary but chose to be a contractor. Therefore, she is self-employed, working more flexible hours.

6. Set a start date and a time frame.

At the age of 80, millionaires don't say, "I should have gone for my dream." If fear is tugging at you, set a start date that makes you feel safe. That in itself is the beginning. Next, set a time frame on how long you are willing to try it.

For example, if you are going to have your own CPA firm, tell yourself that you will try with all your might and your most positive attitude. If you don't have enough clients within six months, you can always go back and work for someone else. There are no failures, only learning experiences! You did the best part, you took the risk. Congratulations!

7. Update yourself.

In order to keep updated, ask yourself when you felt you had closed the big deal. Remember it, and know what it feels like. When you don't get that certain job, ask yourself what you could have done better. When you purchase an item or service, ask yourself if you got the best price. Always improve your skills of buying, selling, and negotiating. When I have an important negotiation coming up, I listen to negotiating audiotapes to tune my techniques before the meeting.

8. Build your support system.

Treat all people with respect. This includes customers, vendors, consultants, and in general, everyone. Don't burn any bridges even if others try to. When you honestly care and like others, the flow of energy to success is easy.

Getting The Money To Start Your Business

You have the idea, the location and the right tools but you don't have enough money. The first step to getting the money is to ask yourself these questions:

- How much money do I need?

- For what purposes do I need the money?

- When will I need these funds?

- How will I repay any funds I borrow?

- Am I willing to share ownership and/or profits with investors, partners or venture capitalists?

What about getting money from the bank? The fact is, most banks don't make loans to start-up businesses. However, here are a few tips that can help you get a bank loan:

- Hire a good CPA who can tell your story in numbers.

- Put a presentation together that involves key employees who have experience and expertise in your line of business.

- Maintain or clean up your credit rating.

- Have ample collateral to offer.

- Cut or eliminate your salary. In other words, don't seek a loan to pay yourself.

If the bank still turns you down, there are other ways to get money to start your business. The man who started Replacements Ltd., a supplier of discontinued china and collectibles, was turned down for a loan.

So with just $5,000, he persuaded the owner of a commercial building to loan him retail space. By placing small ads in magazines, he built a customer base and grossed more than $150,000 in sales in just his first year. Today, he has grossed more than $57 million in sales.

Always look to yourself and your business first for various sources of capital. These are sources which are often overlooked:

- Borrow from a profit-sharing or 401K plan. Take a withdrawal from an IRA.

- Request larger fees or cash up-front for new sales/products/services.

- Obtain a home equity line of credit.

- Obtain a credit line from the bank secured by your equipment and vehicles.

- Get a cash advance on a credit card.

- Sell assets and lease replacement vehicles or equipment.

- Borrow the cash value from your life insurance policy.

- Borrow against rental property you may own.

- Ask parents or relatives for a loan or ask them to co-sign on a loan.

- Ask suppliers for financing assistance.

ACE-Net, the Angel Capital Electronic Network, is a nationwide listing service for small, dynamic and growing businesses seeking $250,000 to $5 million in equity financing. ACE-Net may be accessed under SBA Services on the Small Business Administration home page at www.sba.gov. The Small Business Administration, by the way, is a valuable source for information.

If all else fails, just have the guts to start on a shoestring. Remember, I started with $2,000 borrowed from my grandmother! The rest was done with sheer determination and hard work. Consider me as proof that it can be done!

Because I am a visual person I always look for the pictures in a book. So I picked some photos to share with you.

Family Album...

Lights, camera, action! Terri, a ham at just two years of age.

Terri's mom, Loretta and Terri when the business started in 1979.

Terri, mom and step-dad, Taw.

Terri's dad, Dave, Terri, and step-mom, Nancy.

Mom, Terri and dad.

TERRI'S CONSIGN & DESIGN
FURNISHINGS
_{SM}

A Few Stores

Inside And Out...

Scottsdale, AZ

A franchise store in San Diego.

Tempe, AZ

Terri's TV commercials showcasing some of the stores.

Mesa, AZ

Atlanta, GA

Terri's Executive Staff...

Shelly Santucci with Terri on a 1990 company trip.

Chief Operating Officer, Shelly with Terri in 1999 at the Athena Awards.

Chief Executive Officer, Kevin Crippa
having his hair done in Spain while
on another company trip.

Of course, Marcus Curtis,
President of Terri's Consign
& Design wants his hair done
the same way.

Terri and
the guys in
Madrid, Spain.

Terri's Art Upholstery Co...

Bambi Burke, the sales rep, and Terri with a couple of designed chairs.

Terri and Lorie, the artist, with more of their latest creations.

This chair is a rich purple, a copy in the "Petunia & Blue Larkspur" by Georgia O'Keefe.

This vibrant gold chair is a copy of "The Kiss", by Gustav Klimt

A romantic painting by Van Gogh, "Café Terrace at Night."

New Friends...

Katie Couric and Terri in New York.

Lindsay Wagner shares stories of her and her children's dyslexia with Terri.

Geraldo Rivera and Terri.

Terri's Awards...

Avon president Susan Kropf, Terri and US Small Business
Administrator, Aida Alvarez.

Terri receiving her
Entrepreneur of the
Year Award.

*Shelly, Lorie, Terri, Nancy, and her dad
receiving the Blue Chip Award.*

*Terri wins Athena Award presented by news anchor
Lin Sue Cooney.*

Terri Going National...

Terri being filmed at her house for her appearance on "Oprah."

From left, Terri's friend Mary, Terri's aunt Darla Neal, Karen Neal, Oprah's producer, Ray Dotch, and Terri.

Terri's 1999 appearance on CNN.

Terri speaking at the National Association of Women Business Owners.

6

Become A Master
Of Marketing

quote

"Marketing is to understand that everything is a story to tell. Success is becoming a master storyteller."

Terri L. Bowersock

Be Successful Without A Degree In Marketing

Do you believe marketing takes a college degree or that you need to have been born with a talent? I believe that you only need the willingness to believe you can do it. My marketing skills were self-taught. I studied my industry's and my competition's ad campaigns as well as the retail business in general. I paid close attention to advertising styles and trends and relied on my intuition and creativity to develop campaigns for Terri's Consign & Design. I continually tried new concepts and actively explored media opportunities to make our advertising stand out. Being creative is the real key to marketing on a shoestring.

Here's an example, one Phoenix summer when the thermometer was pushing 110 degrees, we had an authentic polar bear rug come in on consignment. Instantly, I called the media, ran out to the street, threw it over my body and pretended to act like a bear to get people's attention. Although we didn't receive much media attention, we did draw a large number of shoppers. (And I almost passed out from heat exhaustion!)

Another time, we had a big Mother's Day celebration accompanied by decorating seminars, food and beverages. (I ate leftover cocktail weenies for two weeks after that one!) We even had a "Monty Hall— Let's Make a Deal Day." (Tired of being haggled all day, I almost had a mutiny from my sales people!)

I knew I had to get more media creative, because a cocktail weenie eating polar bear was not the exact image my mom thought we should have.

My Beginning Tools For Marketing

Here are a few of the lessons I have learned while marketing and advertising Terri's Consign & Design on a shoestring budget.

1. Learn to spot promotional opportunities.

My secret to mastering marketing is having the ability to see public relations tied into advertising opportunities—as described in Chapter One.

Where can you spot promotional opportunities? Here are a few ideas: listen to talk shows on the radio and book yourself guest spots, join and attend groups and organizations for networking, send out unique news releases, market your expertise through public speaking, or write articles offering your help and knowledge.

The key to real success with promotional opportunities is to bring a personal connection with your business and the public. The more you know about someone or something, the more you feel connected to it. We, as human beings crave sharing and joining with each other. Isn't that the purpose of life, to be connected on a conscious level?

2. Be creative and consistent.

Here are my four simple steps:
First, use creative words to tantalize the buyer. When running classified ads in the daily newspaper and local bargain hunter's papers, I don't just list items for sale. Instead, I tell stories about the items and use descriptive words to elaborate on each piece of furniture. A "brown sofa" becomes a "rich Bombay brown suede sofa, ideal for your expensive taste at a quarter of the retail price." I list the sofa's

new price at $1,200 and Terri's "gently used" price at $498. "Gently used" became our trade-mark and the consistent term we always use.

Second, find a creative way to show the public your prices are the best. My innnovation was to advertise in the display or main section of the newspaper with a classified style ad. I would list pieces for sale in classified format with a display heading and pictures. I wanted to let the public know that we still had great "classified ad" prices.

Third, be consistent with your campaign. I carried the same concept in radio, television, magazines and newspaper, giving weekly updates on the latest treasures that had arrived at Terri's Consign & Design.

And last, establish your niche. What do you want to be known for? For example, our consistent use of "gently used" told the public we had better quality.

Another example, at Terri's Consign & Design is we never have a sale. That is too much like other furniture stores! With our stores, it is simple: shoppers save 50-85 percent every day.

Our loyal customers love it. They never have to worry about missing some special pricing gimmick. We stick with great discounted pricing every day. This provides our business with a style or niche that consumers will recognize.

3. Your location can be an important marketing tool.

Your location gives you a community recognition factor. Terri's Consign & Design moved to its second location next to a large retailer, Costco. Costco's huge parking lot was full everyday with shoppers we could attract to our store.

4. Just because it's never been done doesn't mean you shouldn't do it.

I started thinking about all the car commercials on television. There were even commercials for used cars and then I realized that no one had ever put used furniture on the air. The norm was for used furniture stores to not advertise in anything other than the classified section of the newspapers.

Although no one in the country had tried my "gently used" approach, I decided to break the mold and create television commercials. I'm glad I did. This was nothing short of "genius." Business doubled within two months!

When it's never been done before, it gives you an opportunity to be first. When you are No. 1, the awareness is higher, you have longevity, and more creditability. Being first definitely has built in perks.

5. Know what interests the media.

A key to successful public relations and marketing is to look at all situations and find a newsworthy or interesting angle. For example, in the early 80s when the recession hit, more and more people consigned home furnishings with us in order to make money.

Knowing this trend was newsworthy, I told the media about the savings that consignment offered and how money could be made by consigning at Terri's Consign & Design. Recycling was becoming the "in" thing to do and I highlighted the use/reuse benefit of consignment.

The media picked up the story about "where to buy things cheap" and articles began popping up in local newspapers and magazines. This resulted in radio interviews for me. Now we were prepared to ride out the recession. In fact, we not only made it through the recession, our store went from $100,000 a month in sales to $170,000 a month! Clearly, it pays to know what interests the media and how to get your story told.

6. Constantly ask yourself how you can attract customers.

At Terri's, we've used a wide variety of marketing and advertising tools. Our trucks are traveling billboards stating: *"Trucking to Terri's"...Estate, Gently Used, New, Model Home and Liquidations.... Follow Us!*

We've sent brochures to estate lawyers and divorce lawyers. Our sales staff have worn bright red vests and our delivery crews have worn T-shirts emblazoned with both their name and our store name. I've even used a magnetic stick-on sign on the side of my car.

When our third store opened, we used a door hanger campaign to announce our expansion. We blanketed high-income neighborhoods ($200,000+ properties) offering $20 for residents to come shop with us, no strings attached. Terri's Consign & Design wasn't about to offer a miserly percentage discount—that would be too ordinary!

Getting the company name in front of potential customers is the name of the game.

7. Speak to the community.

While building the marketing and advertising programs for Terri's, I worked and planned ads, public relations, speaking and community involvement.

Public speaking and community involvement were crucial. For example, I began speaking after *Inc. Magazine* honored me as Retail Entrepreneur of the Year in 1992 and asked me to tell my story at a conference. When I was on stage, I realized I was a good speaker. I may not be good at spelling or reading, but boy can I tell my story.

I also started volunteering with community projects. My favorite was serving on the steering committee with the National Orton Dyslexia Society, which provided dyslexics with a help hotline. As a result, I was voted an "International Outstanding Dyslexic" and featured on the

Orton Society's 1997 calendar along with Henry Winkler and Lindsey Wagner.

To add to the momentum and to make sure the store benefited from all this publicity, I started doing paid ads and radio spots saying: "Arizona Woman Builds the Nation's Largest Chain of Consignment Furniture Stores." The ads featured my picture and signature on the side with a note stating: "The truth is I started the company because I could not fill out a job application. I have dyslexia, a learning disability that makes it difficult to read and write. Now 18 years later, we're the largest consignment furniture store in the country. That goes to show if you believe in yourself you can do anything!"

Through the years, Terri's Consign & Design has used a variety of marketing and advertising ideas, some new and others just enhanced versions of the tried and true. What has never changed, however, is my advertising philosophy: *I will work hard and diligently to let others know that I believe in my business; to create customer savings where possible; and to maintain honest and credible relationships with others. I stand by my word at work, with the public and in my advertising materials. Every ad is produced with integrity. I really enjoy seeing people get great bargains every day."*

Public Relations Savvy

Naturally, every one would like the media to print or air positive stories about their business. You can increase the chances of this happening by having public relations savvy.

For starters, you must know if you have news, know how to present it, know who to submit it and know how to work with the media. Here is some information that may be helpful.

1. Know what is and isn't news.

Think about what business news you typically see reported. Does your business have news? Here is a short list of items that may be of interest to the media:

- Cutting edge news of your business

- Opening, selling or merging a business with an out of the ordinary spin

- Hirings/promotions of management personnel

- Landing a major contract

- Participation in community events

- Offering public events or special promotions

- Being "the first" to do or get something significant

2. Submit your news.

Once you have news to share, you can write or call the media. There is no guarantee that your news will be published. You can, however, increase the chances by making sure that your news is based on timeliness, public interest, conflict, human interest or future events.

To submit your news by a phone call:

- First find an editor that you like and respect, then call them to compliment them.

- While networking tell others a few highlights, then get their phone number and ask if you can call them later.

■ Sell your story with *enthusiasm.*

■ Tell your story quickly without any details.

Equally important is your news release. Follow a format that will make it easy for the media to use. Your news release should:

■ Be typed or printed on business letterhead.

■ List a name and contact number in the upper right corner.

■ Include the current date.

■ List a release date or indicate "for immediate release."

■ Be written in inverted pyramid style—This means the first paragraph provides the most vital information while subsequent paragraphs elaborate. Keep in mind that an editor will cut sentences from the bottom.

■ Answer the vital questions of "who," "what," "when," "where," "why" and "how." Give the full name of your business and the names and titles of the owners and involved parties. Describe in one or two short paragraphs what your company is doing that is newsworthy. Give the complete address of your business and any other pertinent sites. Give the date and time the news event happened or will happen. Explain why this news is significant. Include how your business will accomplish the actions and how much it will cost. Supplying background information on your company or yourself may be helpful, too.

■ Double-space with one-inch margins.

■ Indicate "-more" or "-end" at the bottom of each page.

■ Send it either in business envelopes or fax it.

■ Accommodate all deadlines.

■ Add photos when you can.

My best success has been in telephoning the news media with great enthusiasm. I excite them about my story. Through the years I have enhanced and added to it accordingly. My closing line is, "What do you need for me to send to you?" Then, I sincerely thank them, as excited as I was with my very first one. I do everything they ask for promptly.

3. Create a PR notebook.

A three-ring notebook is a handy tool as you develop your public relations activities. I suggest creating a special form or sheet to include in your notebook that will help you think on your feet when a reporter calls. This form should have spaces for you to fill in the reporter's name, publication or company, address, phone and fax numbers, specific shows or features and when they are aired or published, and deadlines you must meet. Include space for your conversation notes, too. Write down what you discussed with the reporter. Ask them what other stories they are working on. You will want to jot down things reporters say about themselves. This will help you establish a relationship.

One reporter and I discovered that we were air force brats and both of us had a history of two-year relationships. We spent time analyzing each other's situation and finally came to the conclusion it was because as kids we moved every two years. I ended up being on the front cover of a national magazine.

4. Build your PR mailing list.

It's important that you know who to contact when you have a newsworthy item. I suggest setting up a mailing list with different categories. For example, the national category would include media outlets such as CNN, the *Wall Street Journal*, "Oprah Winfrey" and others.

Another category would be local media, which includes your area's magazines, newspapers, television stations, radio talk programs and cable TV shows. List the reporters or editors you wish to direct your news to in each category. You will want to include those who specifically cover your industry or business people and promotions.

Your local library can be a great place to start building your PR mailing list. A publication titled *Bacon's Publicity Checker or Editor & Publisher* is a valuable source. You can collect the local information you need by looking for the page in your local newspapers and magazines, which lists the staff and editors. Be sure to put this in your mailing list in your PR notebook.

5. Build solid media relationships.

Editors will know when it is news and when it is simply self-promotional materials. In order to gain an editor's trust, never "cry wolf" with non-news.

Always be honest with your story. Tip them off, when you can, to other stories. They will appreciate your effort and it pays off in the long run.

Now To Get Your "Genius Marketing Degree"

I'm about to reveal to you the genius level of marketing that took a small town girl from Mesa, AZ and put her on the "Oprah" show. I have not attended a class in marketing nor have I read any books about the subject. But, I do have my intuition and 20 years of advertising and creating ideas.

I didn't need a degree in marketing to assure myself that I was good, but I must admit it was rewarding in 1997 when I became the finalist for *Inc. Magazine's* Marketing Masters Award. It was just me and my assistant against 380 advertising agencies. Winning this award felt like I had finally gotten an A on my report card. The one I had never gotten before.

The true secret to "genius marketing" is: *to take every marketing avenue and to merge them all together.*

My style is storytelling. Whether it was for furniture, franchises, upholstery or public speaking, I used my own story of how I built them to be successful. Then I stayed consistent and tied it into all marketing avenues: advertising, awards, articles, media interview and even into my speaking.

115

It's like making a snowball. As it rolls along it picks up bits and pieces, the weight begins to gain speed, the speed increases the size, enough for it to be noticed coast to coast.

Storytelling

Realize that everyone has a story. It is the willingness to share with the public. Here are some examples:

- It might be a story about pioneering. For me being a female entrepreneur has been an inspiration to others.

- Maybe it's something new or exciting. Consignment was new in 1979. Most people didn't even know what the word meant.

- Or your story can have historical value. I often compare myself with stories of other historical dyslexic figures that were successful, like Nelson Rockefeller and John F. Kennedy.

- It could be something society feels compassion about and that affects a large percentage of the population. I have certainly felt compassion from people when I have told my own story of adversity. Dyslexia effects an estimated 20 percent of the population.

- Or is your story an attention grabber, like this book, *Success, It Can Be Yours! How to be a Millionaire by Using Your Determination.*

Whether you use all of the examples of stories like I have, or just expand on one point, it is still a story.

My first big attempt at storytelling was a secret about Mom. Boy was she mad when I told the world about this one. It was the early 80s and Arizona had the highest divorce rate in the country. Fortunately, my mom had gotten one. I turned it into publicity and it became news.

During the recession, I told many stories on how people made money selling on consignment. When Barbara Bush had a campaign on reading disabilities my dyslexia stories really hit big.

My best example was when *Entrepreneur Magazine* called to get a small quote about one of my national awards. My fast talking answer was, "You are the reason I won it. Day and night, I studied your manual on how to run a consignment store. Thank you for making it so easy to read, I'm dyslexic."

With that the reporter said, "Would you mind if I got my editor, we might have a story."

"Oh, not at all," I said as I jumped up and down for joy in my office.

That turned out to be a four-page article worth $80,000 and franchise calls came flowing in.

Articles

My most daring article was having my story in *National Enquirer.* My father said he wouldn't even go into a store to buy that gossipy paper. My executive team was sweating, worried about our image. My response was simple. My true passion is to inspire other learning disabled people and because *National Enquirer* has lots of pictures, what magazine do you think they are reading?

It was this style of storytelling that attracted reporters from around the country to tell my story. *Woman's World, Woman's Own, Opportunity World, Inc. Magazine* several times, *Nation's Business Magazine* several times, *Money Magazine* and many more.

So why are articles so important? It's a great way to advertise on a shoestring budget. The public sees articles in publications as truth. Whereas advertising can be known as misleading. Publicity can even can open the doors for growth for your company. It could bring buyers, investors or even a merger. That spells opportunity. Articles bring you more articles.

TV And Radio Interviews

We have become a society of TV watchers. It seems that our world has become so impersonal. Long working hours and family responsibilities in a fast paced world means less time with neighbors, less time to connect with friends, less time to sit under the stars and drink lemonade. Instead, TV talk shows have become our substitute for social relationships. We seem to know more about what celebrities are doing than who our next door neighbor is. Therefore, we become personally fascinated with celebrities.

I started small with an interview, "Where the Jobs Are" on a public access show. Then came "Farm and Home Show," which was a show on how to buy wood furniture. Then noon news with stories about dyslexia. (I tried TV appearances with articles, and would call the TV stations and ask if they wanted the story too.) Then I went after syndicated news interviews and my story was broadcast across the country. This was coupled with several national radio syndicated talk shows like "Erskine Over Night." From this notoriety, national talk shows started calling, "Jenny Jones," "CNN," and of course, "Oprah."

The key was that I always told the same beginning story. When you are trying to reach millions, you can't confuse them with different stories. Remember, if a small radio station calls you for an interview, say yes. It's great practice and you never know who's listening to lead you to your next interview.

Using Speaking For Public Relations

Speaking To Build Your Company.

I know for most of you speaking in public is your greatest fear. But really it's easier than you think. What helped me the most was when I got over the fear of making a mistake in front of everyone. The turning point came one day as I was speaking to a local Rotary Club. All of a sudden, out of my mouth came the wrong words and the wrong facts. It got me so flustered, I even lost my place on my paper. I quickly grabbed my notes, held them up, and said, "Have you ever tried reading notes written by a dyslexic?" At that moment everyone broke into laughter with me. I found out we are all just human.

I started practicing with a small group at Toastmasters. Then I progressed to small classrooms. If you really want to test your speaking abilities, try it on high school students. I found the best attention grabber was "money." I started with, "If you want to be a millionaire you can." Now I have them a little interested. So I proceed to tell them about all the things I have been able to purchase with money like expensive cars, fun games and lots of toys. Now that I have their attention, I proceed with my real message of how important it is to take learning seriously.

From there my speaking expanded to professional groups, national associations, government agencies, and large corporations like AT&T and USWest, and finally to expos and conferences across the country.

Some Speaking Tips To Help You On Your Way

1. Start with small groups.

Once you get over the initial fright of the number attending, you will find out large groups can actually be easier to speak to. If a few people are having a bad day, it shows more in smaller groups, whereas larger groups have a stronger collective energy to deflect negativity. It takes less effort to make a large group have infectious laughter.

2. Pick out a safe atmosphere.

Speak to audiences with whom you have something in common. In the beginning, I felt more relaxed talking to people who had learning disabilities.

3. Talk about something you are passionate about.

Let the group get excited with you. Try putting your notes down so your spirit can show through. When you are passionate, the audience will feel it.

4. Tell personal stories, especially humorous ones.

When telling a tragic story, it's better to give it a humorous twist. When I talk about wearing my mom out carrying a sleeper sofa to the third floor, I emphasize the incident by actually bending over and holding my back while yelling, "I would rather have skin cancer!" just as she did. It gets a laugh every time.

5. When you make mistakes, let the human side show.

When a mistake happens, tell the audience the truth. It helps you relax and get back on track. You will find the audience appreciates your openness. Using humor makes it even easier. Have some one liners as backup.

How Does Speaking Benefit You?

1. It's great advertising for what you are selling.

How often do you get a captive audience?

2. It shows leadership.

People look to leaders for ideas and inspiration.

3. **It opens the doors for more public relations.**

   When I gave the Avon speech in front of 4,000, 800 of them were reporters. From that I got CNN and several national articles.

4. **The most rewarding benefit of speaking is the feeling you get when you touch someone in some way.**

   Sometimes I hear approving comments in the background, hear someone say, "Amen," or hear laughter. Sometimes I see the audience shake their heads with excitement, show a smile, or even shed a tear. And sometimes after the speech they come up to me with a gentle touch to just say, "Thank you."

   I got a letter from a third grader who was learning disabled. It read, "Terri, you showed me that if I believe in myself, I can grow up to be a baby doctor." As I read this I stopped, sat down and cried. I questioned myself, "I wonder if someone had come to my classroom, would it have made a difference for me?" At that moment I made a promise to myself to keep telling my story.

Awards For Public Relations

Ins And Outs Of Awards

Awards can be a great tool for publicity for you and your business. To start, get a list of the awards given out in your city. You will find them given by associations of professional groups, chamber of commerces and charities. One of my best ways of finding local award givers is to watch the newspaper for announcements and write-ups on the current year's winner. I then call them to find out the procedure to apply for that award next year.

To find national awards, I do one of two things. First, I check with large companies that sponsor awards. Second, I look through national magazines for applications for awards. That is how I won my 1998 Entrepreneurial Woman Award. Office Depot had an ad in a national magazine announcing it.

How To Fill Out An Award Application

1. **When you fill out applications, be brief.**

   I was an award judge because I had won the year before. Not only did I have a hard time reading long applications, but other judges commented on tedious applications that were long and drawn out. Judges smile when it's short and sweet.

2. Put your best stuff first.

What you say in the beginning is capturing their heart. You are setting a tone and creating a vision in their mind of who you are and why they should consider you for this award.

3. Print large.

Make it as easy to read as possible.

4. When you list your accomplishments, do it in list form, not in paragraph form.

It visually has a bigger impact.

5. Make sure you pick the right category for you.

When I started applying for awards, the "overcoming adversity category" opened the doors for me.

6. Be dramatic with your story.

Don't be afraid to take them to a laugh or a tear.

7. Make sure it's grammatically correct.

There are some judges who grade you on how well you fill out the application. It shows them how important it is to you.

Winning awards was not easy for me in the beginning. But true success is never, never, never giving up. I first applied for the Athena Award in 1995, and kept applying every year thereafter. I finally won it five years later in 1999, which was the same year Susan Lucci finally won her Emmy. At the acceptance speech I started with, "Susan and I finally made it."

These seven tools also brought me my national entrepreneur awards. I received triple honors from *Inc. Magazine*, with the Marketing Masters Award in 1998, Socially Responsible Entrepreneur of the Year in 1994, and Retail Entrepreneur of the Year in 1992. In 1998 I received the Entrepreneurial Woman of the Year Award from *Entrepreneur Magazine* and in 1999 Outstanding Female Executive from *Elite Who's Who*.

But truly, the Women of Enterprise Award by Avon was the crème da la crème. Not only did it get me on the "Oprah" show, but their award is a lifetime award. Every year Avon invites all the previous winners back to be honored and to participate in the ceremony. Last year Hillary Clinton gave a speech at the awards.

So Why Are Receiving Awards Worth Your Time?

1. My favorite words, *it's free publicity.*

2. It shows that your company has standards high enough to win awards.

3. Awards are image builders. Your integrity is there for all to see.

4. It gives you celebrity status and credibility when you want media interviews.

5. It shows the public your community value. Many of the awards criteria ask for a list of charities or boards on which you sit, asking what you do to give back to the community. By the way, these are always mentioned at the awards ceremony.

6. Awards put you in touch with the winners circle. You now hang out with other award winners. It is this ability to network that helps ease your climb to success.

What Makes This "Genius Marketing?"

Marketing has many different parts varying from a 20 word classified ad to an international appearance. They are all equally important. No article is ever too small or too big. No appearance is too trivial or too tremendous. No award is too insignificant or too global.

It is public relations mixed with your whole advertising campaign that melts together to become one. As with everything in life, one part can not excel without the help of others. When you truly embody this belief, you have earned your genius marketing degree.

7

Leadership
With
Humanity

quote

"Leadership, you would think, is about getting others to do something for you, but true leadership is when you do something for them. You believe in them."

Terri L. Bowersock

The Importance
Of Leadership

The Wall Street Journal did a survey asking top CEOs what they viewed as the business world's biggest concern for the future. Guess what they said. Leadership! Approximately 55 percent of the top CEOs said management was their top concern.

As a leader, you must get involved and be able to communicate with employees. How you communicate and respond impacts your bottom line. The business leaders of today and the future must realize that employees are the true profit center.

How can you become an effective leader? Take a closer look at the following steps that can help you achieve that goal:

- Prepare yourself.

- Grow in your leadership.

- Integrate heart and soul.

- Share your leadership style.

Prepare Yourself For Leadership

First and foremost, you must be emotionally healthy to be an effective owner, leader or manager. Clear your personal baggage. Don't be the person with an ego problem who orders employees around and is offended if they don't do what they are told. Or the person without enough self-confidence to communicate, causing staff members to get so little guidance that they become "bad employees." Or the manager without self-discipline who comes to work with a hangover or sets a poor example by being exceptionally disorganized.

Start by sitting down and doing a thorough inventory of both your personal and business life. Make a list of your weaknesses and strengths. Know yourself inside and out and take steps to improve. Read books, listen to tapes, get counseling or join groups. Your goal is to become a self-confident leader whose ego is in balance; a leader who can motivate employees to have pride in their work. When your leadership reaches this point, you will have created the vital teamwork that equals success for all.

Grow With Leadership

Once you have established yourself as a leader, be prepared to grow not only your business, but your leadership skills.

The growth of my business was based on leadership. I didn't have a management degree or money to buy my way through mistakes. I learned that it takes hard work to succeed, but you must also learn to work smart.

Think of this as a series of steps. When you start a business or begin to manage one, your own energy and hard work creates success. To continue that success, you must then hire people and build a team to take the business to the next level. You must empower these employees and be enthusiastic about the company. It is important to be a secure person who is not afraid to hire the right people—even people more gifted than yourself or those who have developed the skills you need by working at other companies. Finally, you must understand what leadership is and how to use it. Leadership is not about having power or control. It is about setting examples and sharing enthusiasm.

How do I know about leadership? From my own experience in building Terri's Consign & Design. In the company's early days, leadership was easier for me. I had great, infectious enthusiasm and employees were excited to help build the business together. Before long, I brought in upper level people such as the CEO and COO—people I felt were smarter and more gifted in certain areas than I was. At first, I thought this smart team was better at making decisions and understanding technology. I became afraid to speak up and believed my ideas were inferior. For a year, I felt frustrated and out of control. Then something happened. This team started changing some of the basic principles that the company was built upon.

My CFO felt that the red slash mark we used for monthly markdowns looked like we had made a mistake when pricing the furniture. Contrary to their belief, just ask any great bargain hunter, and you'll know that those slash marks signify even more savings.

Another time, the management team wanted to increase our furniture pickups from seven to ten a day. I had always said that Terri's Consign & Design would pace itself, do a good job and build its success, but not at the expense of our labor force.

In both of these instances, I knew I needed to stand by my principles. I needed to retain those red slash marks, and the reasonable pickup schedule. But I was afraid to speak up. That is, until one day I shared my frustration with a friend.

"Who owns the company," she asked.

"I do," I replied.

I had never really understood what it meant to lead the company. I had always just been one of the team. I had to overcome those feelings that I was inferior and that my ideas were not good or as smart. I had to accept that I, Terri Bowersock, was the leader of the company. I was the one with the true understanding of why people shopped at Terri's Consign & Design. I knew our success was because of our warm, friendly atmosphere, and some very basic rules of consignment selling. Above all, I knew I must protect and maintain that atmosphere and our fundamental rules.

With this in mind, I sat down and wrote Terri's Golden Rules. Representing the principles that the company was founded on, the rules clarified several issues, including: red line mark downs must stay, employees would not work an excessive number of hours, prices wouldn't be hiked up and a store's stock would consist of 70 percent gently used and 30 percent new items.

With these rules, the management team could expand technology and grow the company, but they could not stray from our basic principles.

Next, I held my first board meeting in my dining room. Thanking everyone for the great ideas they had contributed, I stated that I would be supportive of their knowledge and empower each person to use their entrepreneurial spirit to grow the company. I explained that our company was like a tree, and the Golden Rules were the roots responsible for our growth. I asked them to honor and respect these rules as our founding principles. From that day on my leadership grew.

Today, I have the self-confidence to let my management team do its job and the knowledge of when to step in and maintain the vital principles that built Terri's Consign & Design. In the process of growing my leadership, I developed the following leadership rules:

1. Share the values and morals that are the foundation of your business.

This means sharing the philosophy behind your

company. By doing this, employees feel like they are part of the business and know its purpose, rather than being replaceable workers.

2. Test or train using multiple styles.

Remember that we all don't learn the same way. Some may learn by reading a manual, others may need more hands-on learning. Some can be told, others need to be shown. If you give a test, be sure to ask if the employee or job applicant needs assistance. Find out if they have a learning disability. They may need a verbal rather than written test.

3. Have self-control.

You must have self-control before you can expect others to have self-control. The manager who shows up with a hangover certainly will not gain respect when lecturing others for the same behavior.

4. Know the job.

Educate yourself on the daily duties of every department and position you manage. This will give you self-confidence. Others will respect your knowledge and do their best work.

5. Plan the work and set the standards.

Create a daily work plan that will enable your business to reach its goals. Set standards for how the plan will be carried out. Hold employees accountable to the plan. The leader who wavers back and forth with decisions or actions has confused employees! Reward accomplishments and correct poor performance by coaching and re-teaching.

In the early days, I made the mistake of sharing with everyone all my creative ideas. Some of my employees became confused and didn't follow through with the original plans. I quickly learned to only discuss my ideas with a select few.

6. Hire the right person for the job.

As leader, you must know the profile of the right person for a particular job. As a manager, it is your responsibility to guide and teach employees how to excel at their job. If an employee is frustrated or feeling unsuccessful, they may need to be put in another position or seek a job that better suits them.

7. Pay attention to the energy in your company office or building.

Keep in mind that one negative person can influence everyone. Your choices are to either get the negative person thinking and feeling positively or get them off your team. Positive energy grows a business.

8. Visit the village.

The best source of information and insight into productivity is to get out of your office and into the workplace to watch, listen and learn. This can give you an opportunity to see if the plans figured on paper are practical in real work life. If you are wondering how a job can be done better, listen to the people who do it everyday. More often than not, they will have the answer.

9. Be a mentor.

Assume full responsibility for teaching and coaching others. Help people develop the talents needed to achieve their goals. Teach them to be calm and self-assured. When you believe in them, they will believe in themselves. Importantly, you will build loyalty and respect.

10. Roll up your sleeves and help.

The greatest leader is a servant to all. Truly great leaders are willing to do whatever it takes to get the job done.

11. Pay and praise accordingly.

Pay for what employees know and they will learn more. Pay for what they do and they will do more. Praise employees for all to hear and others will want to join in and create an atmosphere where new ideas are welcomed.

12. Give employees the power and authority to do their jobs.

Let employees make mistakes. Mistakes are the stepping stones to success. Don't let the fear of failure crush your employee's enthusiasm. Let them spread their wings and your business will reap the rewards.

For example: when my CEO put his first real estate deal together, he pushed the negotiations too far and lost the deal.

"Did you learn from the mistake?" I asked him.

"Yes," he answered.

"Then so be it," I said.

Since then, this same CEO has had tremendous success in the real estate market and proven himself invaluable to Terri's Consign & Design. In a few short years, he turned a $400,000 piece of land into an asset worth $1.8 million. This gave him the ability to purchase two more buildings for our company using equity with the bank. This success would have not been possible unless he was given the power to take risks and fail with my support.

13. Share the profit.

This is what makes your employees entrepreneurs and what helps them enjoy what they are doing. I gave my CEO a percentage of our real estate profits because his work made those profits possible. Members of my executive team each are given shares in Terri's Consign & Design.

14. Balance your working hours and personal time.

As a leader, it is important to realize that when you balance both your personal and work life, your achievements are greater and the quality of your work is higher. It's also important to make sure that your employees aren't so engrossed in their jobs that their family lives suffer. I've jokingly threatened to take off my shoe and beat anyone working too many hours a week! I've also been known to send employees on vacation.

15. Have a caring personality.

A positive environment starts with you. Working in a pleasant environment makes it fun to come to work. If it becomes a grind, create incentive with rewards. Don't punish with deadlines. Instead, remember that an infectious smile and truly caring about people can create happiness.

16. Keep your eye on the bottom line.

It is great to run a smooth operation with positive attitudes but it must be profitable. As leader, you are responsible for cutting costs or increasing revenues. Know what it costs to open the doors every day. Know the cost for each square foot in the building. Know how to watch the bottom line for profit.

17. Make spirituality a part of your leadership.

Believe that you will succeed by attracting the right people. Seek mentors so that you will learn new things. Eliminate judgement, envy, selfishness, and prejudice. Know that negative attitudes will never bring the right kind of success. Treat all employees equally, regardless of age, sex, race, religion or sexual preference. Respect that all people, plants, and animals are important for our future. Understand that you have a much higher purpose than just money. Keep your ego in check and let the business and employees stand on their own and enjoy the success. Teach humanity by example.

Integrate Your Heart And Soul

In order for your business to be successful, you must take the time to integrate the goodness of your heart and soul into the business. You must understand that the person with the smallest job is equal to the CEO or top manager. Each of us is here for different lessons. You must understand that so you can respect, value and pass no judgment on others.

Consistently incorporate this respect for all people into every decision you make, whether that decision impacts employees, customers or yourself. Use your morals and values. Put yourself in others' shoes and consider the quality of both their work and personal life.

Set good examples. Treat your employees the way you want them to treat your customers. Don't forget that how you treat your managers is reflected in how they treat their employees. How you and others within your business treat each other all influences whether your customers will be satisfied and whether your workplace will be enjoyable.

Kind words and actions have great strength and power. Say "good morning" before you start assigning work or tasks. Take a minute to smile and tell employees how much you appreciate their time and hard work. Reward employees, too. Recognize superior performances, give a thank you card or have an employee lunch. Even having a potluck picnic can be an effective and inexpensive way to spend quality time with employees.

Operate on the belief and understanding that no one is a bad worker or person. They just may not be right for their job. Try moving them to a different position. If necessary, explain that the job doesn't seem to make them happy and that it would be better if they found the right job.

Putting heart and soul into your business is an ongoing process that results in profits.

Share Your Leadership Style

As a business owner, you want to be sure that your managers share your compassionate and caring leadership style. Here is a list of leadership tips I have given to managers at all my companies to help them understand and be consistent with the company's leadership style:

1. Implement good news; don't glorify bad news.

Continually delivering bad news creates bad attitudes. On the other hand, sharing good news lifts people's spirits.

2. The spread of good news comes from the top.

When those at the top freely share good news with employees, those employees will in turn share the news with customers. The end result is sales dollars.

3. Walk the walk and talk the talk.

You must do the kind of work and demonstrate the kind of attitude that you expect from your employees.

4. Use sensitivity and compassion.

Always start a meeting or conversation with a positive, understanding statement. For example, acknowledge that retail is hard work and every employee's time is appreciated. Clear the air and remove blocks first.

5. Present everything positively.

Present new rules or procedures to be adopted by pointing out their positive benefits.

6. Manage from the heart.

Base your actions and decisions on doing the right thing. Use compassion as your guide.

7. Keep communicating.

Maintain a consistent and constant flow of information. Ask for ideas for the upcoming newsletter or nominations for company awards.

8. Project the feeling of quality.

Be proud of what your company sells. We make shoppers feel as if they are walking into a variety of high-end furniture stores all under one roof.

9. Let your career goals be known.

Encourage employees to speak up. Let them know that things change and positions become available or are created as the business grows. Share your career goals. This goes for you and your employees.

10. Live in positive thoughts.

Tell yourself: I am today what I thought yesterday; I am tomorrow what I thought today.

An Enlightened Touch

The following list of leadership terms and characteristics also points out common differences between controlling and enlightened leaders.

CONTROLLING LEADERS	vs.	ENLIGHTENED LEADERS
Objective: control		Objective: change
Relies on order-giving		Facilitating/teaching
Rank		Connections
Knows all the answers		Asks the right questions
Limits and defines		Empowers
Issues orders		Acts as a role model
Imposes discipline		Values creativity
Hierarchy		Networking
Demands "respect"		Wants people to speak up, act up
Performance review		Mutual contract for specific results
Automatic annual raises		Pay for performance
Military archetype		Teaching archetype
Keeps people on their toes		Nourishing environment for growth
Punishment		Reward

Reach up/down	Reach out
Bottom line	Vision
Closed: information = power	Openness
Drill sergeant	Master motivator
Command and control	Empowerment
Little time for people	Infinite time for people
Rigid	Flexible
At the top	In the center
Mechanistic	Holistic
Impersonal/objective	Personal
What we are going to do?	How can I serve you/bring out your best?

Building Dynamic Companies Through Forward Vision

quote

*"Some entrepreneurs are just making their money.
Some are building companies and providing jobs.
Dynamic entrepreneurs are changing the world."*

Terri L. Bowersock

Vision Builds The Company

From the beginning, I had a vision that we were a pioneer in the used furniture industry. My first sale at Terri's Consign & Design was the mirror from my childhood bedroom set.

"I'll take it," the lady said.

"You will?" I asked excitedly. I was so thrilled that the buyer had to remind me to add in the sales tax! Standing before my tin cash box, I told her that it was my first sale. She then signed and dated one of the dollar bills for me to hang on my wall.

From that first sale, Terri's Consign & Design has grown to a multi-million dollar, nationwide business. How? By maintaining the company's forward vision.

For starters, the company was founded on a new idea. We were—and are—a true consignment store. Before Terri's Consign & Design, there were just used shops. Used dealers generally priced at the lowest possible price, and the owner typically only received ten cents on the dollar. At Terri's, however, we price items at the best price and pay consignors 50 percent of the sale. We do all the work—pick up the items, sell them, and promptly send payment.

Another important part of our forward vision is how we have positioned ourselves. Thanks to Mom's insistence, we were "the rich man's thrift shop." Terri's Consign & Design only takes clean, quality, in style, name-brand furnishings. This attracts a high-caliber clientele.

Additionally, our business has always focused on rewarding our customers. We do everything we can to show our shoppers that we believe in what we're doing and that we want their shopping experience to be great. The more the customer feels rewarded, the greater the chance that they will continue to be our customer. In fact at Terri's Consign & Design, we even have customers that pitch in and help when they stop in for their weekly visit!

Entrepreneur's List Of What To Avoid

If you are starting a business, use the following information to help you avoid some common pitfalls. Basically, the primary reasons that businesses fail are:

1. Unfavorable relationships with vendors

2. Poor control over your product's costs and quality

3. Not paying attention to the company's financial information

4. Inadequate control of stock

5. Poor customer relations

6. Not promoting and keeping a good image

7. Not understanding the merchandise

8. Failure to make and act on decisions

9. Illness of a vital person

10. Bad relations with employees

11. Not seeking professional help

12. Lack of tax planning that can reduce taxes

13. Inadequate insurance

14. Poor budgeting

15. Reduced sales momentum

16. Selling goods at too low a price

17. Not enough staff training

18. Failure to deal with competition

19. Inadequate credit control

20. Lack of control of liquid assets

21. Not having enough working capital

22. Expanding without enough capitalization

23. Keeping poor financial records

24. Extending too much credit

25. Borrowing too much or relying too heavily on credit

26. Loss of control through creditor's demands

27. Not enough control over receivables

28. Not foreseeing trends in the market

29. Falling prey to con-artists

How To Contract Consultants

Too often we are easy targets for fast-talking consultants. Believe me, I know! Over the last 20 years, I have paid a great deal of money to consultants who were better at talking before the contract was signed than after.

My first was a franchise consultant who talked about how much money I would make and how he'd take care of everything. He said I needed to fly in a lawyer from San Francisco and a manual writer from Los Angeles. I later learned these people were giving him illegal kickbacks! In truth, qualified lawyers and writers are available right in my hometown of Phoenix for half the price. After a year, he walked away with $100,000 and I learned that not all consultants have good intentions.

The next two consultants I turned to used the "I'm your personal friend" tactic. I gave all my media and advertising business to one, who acted as a father figure because he knew that my parents had separated. My payment to him was supposed to cover advertising bills from TV stations. When he failed to pay the stations, I ended up paying twice! The next consultant had been in the antique business and told me I was "the daughter she never had." My mother had just gotten out of the business, so I was an easy target for this one! I paid her up-front, only later to discover that she wanted to completely change the image that had made Terri's Consign & Design successful.

Despite these instances, I still get taken from time to time because my passion to do something overrides my common sense. For example, a fancy-suited gentleman dazzled me with his accomplishments after I decided to become a national speaker. I signed his contract but quickly learned that he was too busy for my calls and offered very little help. He even came to one meeting and started working on the project he should have already completed!

Throughout all this, I have learned some important lessons: know when you really need help; know how much help you need; keep it useful to you and your company; and know how to legally terminate a consultant. Here's a check list that may help when you're hiring a consultant:

- Sign a contract. If your arrangement doesn't work out, a consultant can still make a case that there was a verbal commitment. Without a written contact you cannot prove the terms of business.

- Create your own boilerplate contract with terms that benefit you, such as a three-day notice of cancellation. Compare it against any contract presented to you. Don't sign another's contract unless it is the same as your terms.

- Don't sign any contract immediately. Take time to think about it. I always say that I have to run it by my legal counsel to minimize any high pressure sales pitches.

- Learn enough about the consultant's area of expertise in order to make a good decision. Knowing nothing about franchising made it easy for a consultant to sell me untruths.

- Interview at lease three consultants to find the one that is the best fit for you and your business.

- Be in control. Review and give the final okay for any outside people the consultant wishes to bring in on the project.

- Keep it business. Letting a consultant become a friend or family figure can let them control you on an emotional level, plus make it hard to use your good business sense. Don't let your passion to accomplish something cloud reality.

■ When possible, use a third party to negotiate the contract. This will eliminate the consultant playing on your emotions.

■ Have a "dating" period consisting of several meetings or a short-term agreement before signing a long-term contract. Try not to pay in advance.

■ Make sure you get action. Don't settle for just talking or a teaching lesson. Get what you need to practically set your plans in motion. Actions speak louder than words.

Time Management

A dynamic company is based on a balance of personal time and business time. The demands of running a new business can make time management skills crucial. Following are a few of the lessons I've learned, which may be helpful.

1. Become a list maker forever.

Every morning, make a list of the tasks you need to get done. Rank them by their importance, with A being the most important, B being the second-most important and so on. This will help keep you organized and keep you on track throughout the day.

2. Keep your desk, workspace and home organized.

Psychologically, a disorganized area makes you feel exhausted because you see how much work there is to organize or do. Pick one area to organize every day. Soon, your entire work area will be organized and easier to work in.

3. Make it a habit to finish one project before starting the next one.

Know how big a workload you can handle and still have a life outside of work! Then commit to finish the small tasks or break large projects into manageable tasks to be completed over a period of time. Book any new projects to be done after you have finished the projects already on your plate. This will enable you to maintain a good energy level and avoid disappointing others when you don't get done what you'd promised to get done. Show you know how to manage your projects and do a great job.

4. Deal with the mail as you open it.

Don't just make piles. You'll only end up sorting through the same mail over and over. File, respond or trash each piece of mail when you open it.

5. Plan your leisure time for the year.

Make a list of ideas and take a vacation. Burn out is big in America. You are like a battery and need to be recharged regularly. By the way, some of my best ideas were created when I was relaxed and rested.

6. Learn to one-stop shop.

Whether stopping by the dry cleaner, drug store or grocery store, plan your errands so that you can meet as many needs as possible in one trip. Keep an ongoing list at home of items you need to pick up. I use a grease board in the hall so I can just fly by and jot something on the list. Then when I go shopping, I remember to get everything in one trip rather than repeated trips.

7. Learning and waiting go together.

Keep tapes in your car to listen to during traffic jams. Have a book ready to read while waiting for your appointment at the doctor's office or other places.

8. Be ready for special occasions.

Find a great discount card store and stock up on a variety of birthday, wedding, get well and other cards. Watch for sales and create a stock pile of gifts for last minute giving.

9. Schedule all of your health check ups in the month of your birthday.

No more trying to remember when the last time you saw the dentist was! Mother taught me this one!

10. Learn to say no to unorganized people who want someone like you to help them.

Take care of yourself. Know how much extra time you have and pick the projects that you want to help with—not just the ones others are tossing at you. Energy is important to success. Don't let negative people drain you. You know the kind. They call you up just to complain!

11. Exercise and eat healthy.

Try to eat regularly and plan good healthy meals ahead of time. Exercise will keep your energy at its peak. Taking care of yourself will save you the time wasted if you become ill.

The Foundation That Builds Your Company

1. Help customers save money.

This is my primary goal in running all my companies. Everytime we spend a dollar foolishly, it comes out of our customer's pockets. Every dollar we save our customers puts us another step ahead of the competition. Passing great deals along to our customers is their reward for doing business with Terri's.

2. Keep expenses down.

Everyone at Terri's Consign & Design is committed to minimizing expenses. We have achieved our industry's lowest ratio of expenses to sales. Having the best prices in the furniture business is our reputation. We also pride ourselves on investing to better our employee's jobs and to provide comfortable, convenient locations for our customers.

3. Work smart and be your best.

Don't burden yourself with addictions that rob your energy. Laugh and enjoy your work. Keep your life balanced. The key to success is not to be a workaholic.

4. Maintain a passion for what you are doing.

This is something I do especially in the areas of marketing and studying the competition. I want to know what is available in the market-place, what the prices are, and what's new in terms of style. The goal for Terri's Consign & Design is to be the best place to buy the right look at the best price. I always have my marketing hat on, too, so that I can share my passion for my business.

5. Keep your pipeline full of small projects.

Don't just be an opportunist going for "the big one" that's going to make you rich. Too often, this means waiting for the grand payoff, mean-while however, the monthly bills keep stacking up. It's like a primer on a water pump. When the pipe is kept full of water, it's easy to keep getting water. But when the pipeline is empty, it's much harder to prime it and get the water flowing when you really need it. Simply put, keep doing the small projects. When you have a steady flow of big projects through your pipeline, you can let the small projects go.

How To Become A Team Coach

1. **Set monthly goals, then break them down to weekly and daily goals.**

    Write goals down so that they are not just a verbal commitment. Use a big calendar, grease board or big sheet of paper for all to see. Keep track of the progress so you can say to employees, "Just $5,000 to go, you can do it!" That's your scoreboard.

2. **Have before and after meetings just like a football team getting ready for the big game.**

    At the before meeting, set goals, discuss ways

to close deals, and encourage the whole team to share new ideas. At the end of the day or week, bring the team back together to share open, honest feedback. As the coach, help get everyone talking and learning what they need to know to achieve the sales goals. Sharing ideas helps build team support.

3. On extra busy days, set out a game plan.

Everyone on the team should know their own personal responsibilities, how to be a team player, and what to do when the flood gates open.

The coach's responsibility is to keep the flow smooth, going in the same direction, and informative. Coaches act as cheerleaders keeping the spirit up, a band leader keeping the rythm smooth and an umpire to call time out.

4. Create a sales game for each day of the week.

This will increase the fun and challenge. Competitive play can be rewarding for employees, especially during slow times.

5. **Make sure the playing field is ready.**

    Check that all the elements are in place so that you don't spend the day trying to find them. See if there is anything that needs to be repaired, to be moved or to be completed. Finally, make sure your team is knowledgeable about the product. Are there any great stories they should know to help win the game?

Building A Great Company Through Forward Thinking

Terri's companies have been built on a "human" way of doing business. I have worked to build the business one customer and one employee at a time, using compassion and non-judgment for all.

Sharing our philosophy empowers our employees. We greet each of them with the following:

"We're glad you chose Terri's as the stage to set and achieve your professional goals. You will find that your experience here will not only help you exceed your professional goals but will strengthen your personal goals as well.

Use your good judgment in all situations. Please feel free to ask your manager, or operational managers any question at any time."

This is a business approach that has built not only Terri's companys' success and reputation, but great respect from its workers. Terri's employee Leon Benlezrah says, "This company gives me the freedom to help customers in every way. No one tells me that there is only one way to do my job. I can explore new avenues of enhancing my job, thus strengthening my initiative and business approach."

Clearly, our success is due at least in part to conducting business the human way. We have incorporated the belief in letting employees be their own entrepreneur. That means making mistakes and learning from them. This has kept us a forward thinking company.

How? We don't expend a great deal of time and energy checking up on employees and holding them accountable for dozens of rules. As a result, each person has the time and freedom to expand their department and come up with new ideas.

Stay Open to Opportunity

At first, Terri's Consign & Design was my only business and I thought staying focused on this one business was the way to big success. Like many, I wasn't sure of my abilities to diversify. However, I was exposed to new opportunities as people with many different backgrounds and talents joined the company and were encouraged to act as entrepreneurs. Together with my executive employees, today I am the owner of five different companies.

This includes Terri's Consign & Design Furnishings (eight retail stores), Terri's Consign & Design Franchise (seven franchise stores), Terri-K's Investment Corporation (a real estate company), Terri's Publishing & Speaking (book, audio tape and speaking engagements), and Art Upholstery (furniture with art).

Art Upholstery is a great example of staying open for opportunity. Jane ann had been our buyer and decorator for many years. One day she mentioned that one of her best sofa manufacturers was struggling to survive. Receptive to opportunity, I invested in his sewing machines and now run the upholstery company while he gets a share of it. The best part is that we are able to provide our latest styles (furniture that looks like art) for less because we manufacture it ourselves!

Another example of staying open to opportunity is our most recent idea. This idea stems from our efforts to find a new computer software system to replace our existing, non-user friendly system. During this process, my management team and I discovered that no one had a consignment software program that could handle the needs of our coast-to-coast stores. Additionally, some current furniture software packages were going to be obsolete in five years.

With this in mind, we are planning to create our own software package tailored to our own company rather than using the money to buy an unsatisfactory program. Our goal is to ultimately market this software to other furniture retailers. When this happens, we will have met our own technological needs, plus created a new source of revenue!

Importantly, these companies are all intertwined and support each other. By learning to be open to opportunities, Terri's Consign & Design was able to find the right companies to merge with or purchase.

This created mutually beneficial deals based on trust and a good reputation—not to mention greater success for our business. ■

conclusion

I hope I've inspired you to live your dream and know you can do anything when you believe it. Even though I have not read but a handful of books in my lifetime, I believed I could write a book. It wasn't easy, not being computer literate or even typewriter capable. This book was totally handwritten. An editor was hired just to transcribe my spelling, grammar, and handwriting. *So if a girl who flunked spelling can write a book, you can do anything you want to do.*

As I have ended every speech, so I will end the book. You and I are fortunate to live in America—truly the land of opportunity—where you can be a millionaire or even an author...no matter what race, sex, age, religion, or disability.

Famous People with Learning Disabilities

It is important for dyslexics to know that their learning disability is a challenge that can be dealt with, and more importantly, that it has nothing to do with intelligence. Being dyslexic does not mean you are dumb! For proof, consider the following list of outstanding individuals who, by the way, happen to be dyslexic.

Harry Belafonte
(Singer/actor/producer/
entertainer/human rights
activist)

Chastity Bono
(Singer/daughter of Sonny
and Cher)

Neil Bush
(Businessman/son of former
President George Bush and
wife Barbara)

Cher
(Entertainer/actress/singer)

Agatha Christie
(Mystery writer)

Tom Cruise
(Actor)

Walt Disney
(Cartoonist/creator of TV shows
and movies, Disneyland and
Disney World Theme Parks)

Thomas Edison
(Inventor/scientist)

Albert Einstein
(Physicist/writer)

Dwight Eisenhower
(U.S. President/five-star
military general)

F. Scott Fitzgerald
(Writer)

Gerald Ford
(U.S. President/U.S. Congressman)

Danny Glover
(Actor)

Tracey Gold
(Actress)

Whoopi Goldberg
(Oscar-winning actress/comedian)

Malcolm Goodridge, III
(Senior Vice President of American Express Corp.)

Bruce Jenner
(Olympic decathlon gold medallist)

Magic Johnson
(Olympic gold medallist/basketball player/AIDS activist)

John F. Kennedy
(U.S. President/U.S. Senator/author)

John Lennon
(Musician/member of the Beatles)

Jay Leno
(Comedian/entertainer/television talk show host)

Charles Lindberg
(Aviator/author)

Olaf
(King of Norway)

George Patton
(Five-star military general)

Nelson Rockefeller
(U.S. Vice President/Governor of New York)

Nolan Ryan
(Former baseball player)

Charles Schwab
(Businessman/founder of Parents' Educational Resources Center)

Tommy Smothers
(Singer/musician/comedian/entertainer)

Jackie Stewart
(Professional race car driver)

Patrick Swayze
(Actor/dancer/horse breeder and trainer)

Leonardo da Vinci
(Inventor/artist/sculptor/architect/scientist)

William Westmoreland
(Four-star military general)

Robin Williams
(Actor/comedian)

Charles Windsor
(Prince of Wales)

Henry Winkler
(Actor/director/producer)

Virginia Woolf
(Writer)

Loretta Young
(Actress)

Terri L. Bowersock

Besides keeping busy with being the president and owner of five businesses, Terri spends her time supporting learning disabilities, environmental issues, human rights and women in business.

Her newest venture is setting up Terri's Learning Disabilities Fund with an annual award ceremony to bring more awareness to this hidden disability. All funds go to schools, organizations, and prisons, to benefit both children and adults.

Terri has lived in the Phoenix metro area for the last 28 years spending time with family, friends, and her cats, Lilly and T.C.

Store Locations...

Phoenix, AZ (6 stores)
Las Vegas, NV (3 stores)
Orange County, CA (1 store)
San Diego, CA (2 stores)
Tucson, AZ (1 store)
Atlanta, GA (2 stores)
Denver, CO (1 store)

Interested in a Terri's Consign & Design Franchise?

Terri's is the largest consignment furniture chain in the country. If you would like to own a Terri's Consign & Design franchise in your city, please call (800) 455-0400. Information will be sent to you.

About Speaking

For more information about Terri speaking for your organization, call toll free (877) 393-5656.

Interested in Art Upholstery?

If you would like to know more about furniture that looks like art, call toll free (877) 393-5656.

ORDER FORM

Telephone Orders: **Postal Orders:** Terri's Publishing & Speaking
Toll Free (877) 393-5656   1826 W. Broadway #4 • Mesa, AZ 85202

Success *It Can Be Yours!*
by Terri L. Bowersock

Please send _____ copies of the book, *Success* *It Can Be Yours!* at $12.00 each plus $3.50 shipping per book. (Arizona residents add .86 per book for sales tax).

Name: _____

Address: _____

City: _____ State: _____ Zip:_____

Telephone: (_____) _____

Payment (US Funds Only)

❏ My check or money order for $ _____ made out to "Terri's Publishing & Speaking" is enclosed.

❏ VISA   ❏ MASTERCARD   ❏ DISCOVER   ❏ AMERICAN EXPRESS

Card Number: _____

Name on Card: _____ Expiration Date: _____

Signature: _____